It Happened
In Iowa

It Happened In the West Series

It Happened In Iowa

Remarkable Events That Shaped History

Tammy Partsch

TWODOT®

GUILFORD, CONNECTICUT
HELENA, MONTANA

A · TWODOT® · BOOK

An imprint of Globe Pequot
An imprint and registered trademark of Rowman & Littlefield

Distributed by NATIONAL BOOK NETWORK

British Library Cataloguing in Publication Information Available

Library of Congress Cataloging-in-Publication Data

Names: Partsch, Tammy, author.
Title: It happened in Iowa : remarkable events that shaped history / Tammy
   Partsch.
Description: Guilford, Connecticut : TwoDot, [2017] | Includes
   bibliographical references and index.
Identifiers: LCCN 2016057257 | ISBN 9780762764402 (pbk.)
Subjects: LCSH: Iowa—History, Local. | Frontier and pioneer life—Iowa. |
   Iowa—Biography.
Classification: LCC F621.6 .P37 2017 | DDC 977.7—dc 3 LC record available at
   https://lccn.loc.gov/2016057257

♾️™ The paper used in this publication meets the minimum requirements of American National Standard for Information Sciences—Permanence of Paper for Printed Library Materials, ANSI/NISO Z39.48-1992.

Printed in the United States of America

CONTENTS

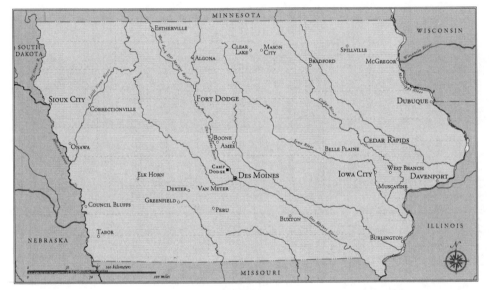

IOWA

CONTENTS

ACKNOWLEDGMENTS

Special thanks go to:

Kris and Joy at the Iowa Aviation Museum in Greenfield. Your passion for your museum was inspiring!

Deb at the Danish Windmill in Elk Horn. You were so helpful, kind, and knowledgeable.

The friendly staff at the Iowa State Historical Society Library.

Amy Allgood and Pam Frana for letting me take time off to write. You gals are the best!

Mom and Dad for instilling in me a love of history, a desire to learn, and the courage to take the road less traveled.

Luke for, well, just being Luke. I thank God for you every day . . . and I love you more.

Finally, Dave for being my driver, my sounding board, and my sweetie pie. Mmm-wah.

INTRODUCTION

There is an iconic scene in the movie *Field of Dreams* that every Iowan knows. The sun is setting over the cornfields of Ray Kinsella's farm as he is asked the famous question: "Is this heaven?" Ray smiles slightly and simply responds, "It's Iowa."

From its rolling plains to its urban centers, Iowa is many things to many people. Geologists are in awe of the Loess Hills in the west while anthropologists examine the Effigy Burial Mounds in the east. Computer science majors flock to Iowa State University, while art enthusiasts visit Grant Wood's studio in Cedar Rapids. More than 90 percent of Iowa's land is dedicated to farming and feeding the people of the world.

Iowa is also home to its share of quirky events and people. Nowhere else in America will you find the National Hobo Convention (Britt) or a National Skillet Throwing Contest (Macksburg). Where else but Villisca can you stay the night in a house that was once the scene of a gruesome unsolved mass murder? And who can debate the distinctiveness of the football field–size Grotto of the Redemption in West Bend?

These places, along with those explored in this book, are what make Iowa unique. But even more so are the people. From Iowa's early explorers and settlers to today's movers and shakers, Iowa has a history of leaving her mark on the people she comes into contact with, just as those same people leave their mark on Iowa.

The rest of that conversation in *Field of Dreams* is usually forgotten, but after the exchange about Iowa and heaven comes another thunderbolt. John Kinsella, Ray's father and the man who asked the original question, tells Ray that heaven is the place where dreams come true. Ray looks around at his farm and at his wife and daughter giggling on the porch swing. He realizes that perhaps he is in heaven after all. He is at home in Iowa.

DUBUQUE LEAD MINES

1788

Julien Dubuque stood on a bluff high above the Mississippi River. He looked down at the river below him and then turned to face west. The September sun was setting behind the soft hills in front of him; this was now his land. While he appreciated the beauty of the land, he was more interested in what was hidden beneath the ground.

Dubuque was born in 1762 and raised in the Quebec province of Canada. Fluent in both English and French, Dubuque earned his keep as a fur trader in Canada and the upper midwest US territories. In the early 1780s, Dubuque heard a rumor of bountiful lead in the Spanish-owned lands just west of the Mississippi River. Making his way downriver, Dubuque found himself among the Mesquakie Indians, with whom he soon became friends.

Now it was 1788 and Dubuque had just made an agreement with Mesquakie chief Aquoqua that would allow Dubuque the right to mine on about twenty-one acres of Mesquakie land near the mouth of Catfish Creek. The Mesquakies had mined lead for generations and used a ground powder form of the natural resource to make black paint. They used the paint for body and face decoration during times of war and celebrations. French explorers who came to the area in the early 1700s taught the Indians how to smelt the ore and shape it into tools and utensils. In recent years, the Mesquakies had been trading lead ore to the French for guns and knives. In this way, lead became the first exportable natural resource for what is now Iowa.

The twenty-six-year-old Dubuque was trusted by the Indians. He treated them courteously and honestly, and they responded in kind. In addition to allowing Dubuque to mine on their land, they actually assisted him with the operation.

When Dubuque opened his mines in 1788, he brought ten French Canadians with him to the area. They mingled with the four hundred residents of the Mesquakie village, one hundred of whom were warriors. While the French Canadians worked the mines as overseers and smelters, Dubuque recruited the Mesquakie women and old men, not warriors, to work in the mines. The miners used hoes, shovels, pickaxes, and crowbars to dig long trenches in the ground. The trenches sloped gradually deeper into the hillside. The miners walked into the mines with large baskets, chipped out chunks of lead from their horizontal deposits, and brought the baskets full of lead back out of the mine. The lead was then melted down to remove impurities, and poured into wooden molds to cool into bars.

In 1796, perhaps feeling nervous that he was mining on land that was actually claimed by Spain, Dubuque traveled to New Orleans to meet with the Spanish governor of Louisiana, Francisco Luis Hector de Carondelet. Dubuque's aim was to receive official permission from the Spanish monarchy to continue his mining operation. By this time, Dubuque's mines stretched twenty-one miles up the west side of the Mississippi River and nine miles inland.

Dubuque came into the meeting with Carondelet with an ace up his sleeve. He asked to obtain a land grant to continue his mining operation in what he was now going to call the "Mines of Spain." The pandering worked, and Dubuque was given the land grant.

Back upriver, work in the mines continued. Over the years, many of Dubuque's workers married Indian women. Soon the area was filled with cabins, farms, fences, a mill, a smelting furnace, a smithy, and a trading post. Dubuque, who was quickly becoming a very wealthy man, would take boatloads of furs, hides, and trinkets downriver to St. Louis a couple of times a year. He relished the culture he found in St. Louis during these visits and was often found at balls and concerts.

Also while in St. Louis, Dubuque began a friendship with that city's founder and wealthy fur trader, Auguste Chouteau. That friendship turned professional in October 1804 when Dubuque, faced with mounting debts due to a lavish lifestyle and generous habits, sold nearly half of his land to Chouteau. Dubuque continued to mine, trade, and farm under the eye of Chouteau, but never financially recovered. Dubuque passed away at the age of forty-eight on March 24, 1810.

Dubuque was buried with full tribal honors in a bluff overlooking the Mississippi River near the mouth of Catfish Creek. Members of the Mesquakie tribe erected a wooden shelter above the grave. That shelter was replaced in 1897 by a twenty-five-foot-tall limestone late Gothic Revival tower that suggests a castle.

The Mines of Spain was renamed the Dubuque Lead Mines. Other white settlers attempted to continue to mine on Dubuque's land, but the Mesquakie Indians refused to honor their claims, declaring the land to be theirs again. After a legal battle, the United States took control of the land and put it under the jurisdiction of the US Army. It was not legal to settle in Iowa until the 1830s, but by 1829 more than four thousand mining permits had been issued for the area. In 1833, the area received its official charter, and the obvious choice for a city name was Dubuque.

Today, the area where Dubuque started mining is known as the Mines of Spain Recreation Area. It is estimated that there are close to two thousand abandoned mines in and around Dubuque today. Julien Dubuque is remembered as a refined intellectual, an adventurous entrepreneur, and perhaps the first permanent white settler in Iowa.

THE DEATH OF SERGEANT FLOYD

1804

In late spring of 1803, a series of signatures on a document in Paris changed the course of American history. The document in question outlined the details of the Louisiana Purchase, a deal between France's Napoleon Bonaparte and US president Thomas Jefferson that doubled the size of the United States.

Even before the ink was dry, President Jefferson asked his private secretary, Meriwether Lewis, to lead an expedition into the wilds of the Louisiana Purchase. Lewis agreed, and enlisted his old US Army mate William Clark to share command of the expedition.

Lewis and Clark spent the rest of 1803 and the first part of 1804 recruiting strong, single men for the expedition, men who would be able to survive the hardships that they were sure to face on the journey. Many of the men who were chosen had served in the US Army in some capacity, and most had good hunting and shooting skills. By May 1804, after gathering supplies and crafting a large keelboat that they planned to use to maneuver up the Missouri River, the Corps of Discovery was ready to go.

One of the first men to volunteer for duty on the expedition was Charles Floyd. Floyd, who was born in Kentucky and a distant relative of William Clark, was twenty-two years old at the time of the expedition. Lewis and Clark made Floyd a sergeant in the Corps; he was one of three sergeants appointed by Captains Lewis and Clark.

The Corps was a team of just over thirty men when it set out from St. Louis, Missouri, in May 1804. During their round-trip covering more than eight thousand miles across the Louisiana Purchase and the uncharted territory in the extreme northwest of what is now the United States, they would travel by keelboat, canoe, horse, and on foot.

At the end of the journey in 1806, after Lewis, Clark, and the Corps had reached the Pacific Ocean and made their way back to civilization, they were not the same company that had left two and a half years previously. Men had left the expedition at certain points to return downstream with flora and fauna collected along the way, and at one point a Shoshone woman named Sacagawea, along with her French trapper husband, Toussaint Charbonneau, and their newborn son, joined the company.

The Corps was also missing Sergeant Charles Floyd.

All was going well for the expedition as they entered their fourth month of travel in 1804. There had been no big surprises as they traveled west across what is now Missouri and then north. They saw their first Native Americans in late July or early August. On August 2 a few Indians from the Oto and Missouri tribes visited the expedition's camp, and, in the first face-to-face contact the Corps had with Indians, the Oto and Missouri men were given tobacco, pork, flour, and meal by Lewis and Clark. In return, the Oto and Missouri tribes sent the Corps fresh watermelon.

The next day, August 3, 1804, the Corps of Discovery had their first official meeting with tribal leaders at a place they called Council Bluffs, in present-day Iowa. Lewis spoke to the tribal leaders about their new "Great Chief" (President Jefferson). The Corps distributed trinkets, whiskey, and gunpowder to the tribesmen. While the men of the Corps weren't sure that their intentions were understood, they all felt relieved that the first meeting ended peacefully.

After the meeting at Council Bluffs, the Corps of Discovery loaded their keelboat and turned the prow north again.

Two weeks later, on August 18, 1804, the Corps spent the evening hours celebrating Meriwether Lewis's thirtieth birthday. After a long day of pulling themselves up the Missouri River, they all gladly tossed back an extra swallow of whiskey before dancing around the fire.

Sergeant Charles Floyd did not participate in the dancing. He had been in considerable pain all day. It started as a dull pain in his stomach, but now he was experiencing sudden cramping. He had no desire to eat any of the salted pork and beans that had been served for dinner. He felt like vomiting just thinking about it.

The next day, August 19, Sergeant Floyd didn't feel any better. In fact, the dull pain in his stomach had moved to his lower right abdomen and increased in pressure. Both Lewis and Clark took turns looking Floyd over. Clark diagnosed a case of bilious colic and tried to make Floyd comfortable.

Just after two o'clock the next afternoon, on August 20, Floyd lay in the keelboat, surrounded by his fellow Corps members. Floyd turned slightly to Lewis and said that he was going away. Sergeant Charles Floyd died with, as Lewis recorded in his journal that night, "a great deal of composure."

The members of the Corps of Discovery pulled the keelboat over to the east side of the Missouri River. Securing the boat to sturdy trees along the riverbank, they carefully carried the shrouded body of Sergeant Floyd along a small tributary to the top of a nearby hill and buried him overlooking the Missouri River. Lewis spoke the service, and Floyd was buried with Honors of War.

After the solemn service, a red cedar post was erected at the head of the grave. One member of the Corps engraved Floyd's name, title, and the date on the post. As the men made their way back down the hill to the keelboat, they decided to name the hill Sergeant Floyd's Bluff. The small tributary was named Floyd's River.

Sergeant Charles Floyd was the first person in the Corps of Discovery to die. What is astounding, though, is that Sergeant Charles Floyd was the *only* person in the Corps who died during that long, arduous trip. Modern research into Floyd's symptoms as described by Lewis and Clark in their journals leads scholars to believe Floyd died of a ruptured appendix, a condition that was unknown—and therefore fatal—at the time.

When the Corps of Discovery came back down the Missouri River in 1806, they made a point to stop at Sergeant Floyd's Bluff to visit the grave. They found the site had been disturbed, either by animals or Indians, so they reburied him.

Fifty years later, Sergeant Floyd's resting place was officially in the northwest corner of the state of Iowa, near the town of Sioux City. In 1857, a flood caused a portion of Sergeant Floyd's Bluff to collapse and exposed the grave. Sioux City residents moved the body approximately six hundred feet back from the river's edge and talked of erecting a more permanent structure. A one-hundred-foot-tall sandstone obelisk was completed in 1901. The remains of Sergeant Charles Floyd are interred inside.

The Lewis and Clark Expedition opened the West for US expansion and settlement. Someone like Sergeant Charles Floyd would have been a fitting example of an early Iowa pioneer. As Clark said, with his loose grasp of the laws of spelling, "This Man at all times gave us proofs of his firmness and Deturmind resolution to doe Service to his Countrey and honor to himself."

GRAND MORMON ENCAMPMENT

1846

By the time the first Mormons reached the Missouri River in 1846, they were on the verge of collapse. The 250-mile trek across the Iowa Territory that was supposed to have taken a few weeks instead took four months. The Mormons, escaping persecution after the mob murder of their founder and leader, Joseph Smith, in Nauvoo, Illinois, had crossed the Mississippi River into Iowa Territory in February 1846. The plan was to make it to the Rocky Mountains before winter and then to continue on to their new home in Utah.

Before leaving Nauvoo, each Mormon family was given a team, a wagon, a tent, food, a rifle, and seed. They packed up what belongings they could and headed west.

Now it was already mid-June, and the leaders knew they had run out of time. To survive the winter in the Rockies meant getting there in enough time to build shelters and lay in stores of venison and produce. That would not happen this year.

Late winter weather and heavy spring rains had slowed the migration of twelve thousand people, three thousand wagons, and thirty thousand head of livestock. Even as the first batch of settlers, led by Brigham Young and Orson Hyde, had reached the far western side of Iowa Territory, thousands of Mormons were still scattered along the trail across the territory behind them.

Young and Hyde decided to halt the migration at that point and set up two semi-permanent camps to house their brethren. Young and several select families crossed the river at that point and set up what they called Winter Quarters. Hyde stayed in Iowa Territory and gathered his men to start creating a Grand Encampment.

Hyde named his settlement Kanesville. Buildings were erected and crops were planted in preparation for the rest of the Mormons following them from Illinois. In the late 1830s, Hyde had been one of a small group of Mormon missionaries who had traveled to England to spread the gospel. Because of Hyde's connections to the Mormon Church in Britain, with its nearly thirty thousand members, he and Young also knew that thousands of Mormon immigrants from Europe would soon be arriving as well, so they designed Kanesville to be more permanent than a regular camp.

Within a year there were approximately 350 log cabins in Kanesville, plus a post office and retail stores. The Mormons missed the $1 million temple they had built back in Nauvoo and made the decision that Kanesville would not be complete without a tabernacle. Work began in the fall of 1847, and the temple was completed in three weeks. However, when spring arrived the next year, water started to come up through the floor of the tabernacle. Because the ground had been frozen when the building was erected, the builders had no way of knowing that they had built the tabernacle over a spring. In addition, the timbers used in the construction had not been given enough time to dry out and now were starting to shrink. That first tabernacle had to be dismantled.

Young's Winter Quarters across the river in what is now Omaha was abandoned in April 1847. Young and nearly 150 others, only three of whom were women, hitched up their wagons again to continue the trek to Utah. Hyde and the rest in Kanesville were instructed to stay there as support for the Mormons who would be arriving later.

Many of the struggles Hyde faced early on in Kanesville were due to a lack of manpower. In 1846, America was fighting in the Mexican-American War. Brigham Young encouraged able-bodied men to form a Mormon Battalion and join in the effort. Five hundred young men, those needed most for constructing the new encampment, left Kanesville and marched to war.

The Mormon Battalion received money for uniforms, but most of them sent the funds back to Kanesville. They marched first from Kanesville south to St. Joseph, Missouri, then to Fort Leavenworth, Kansas, then southwest to Santa Fe, New Mexico. From there, they marched to Tucson, Arizona, before finally making it to San Diego, California. By that time the Mormon Battalion had marched two thousand miles and hadn't seen any fighting—and they never would, as the Mexican-American War was over.

After the Mormon Battalion was discharged in the summer of 1847, they stayed in California to help dig wells and make bricks for new settlements there. In time, some came back to Kanesville, but many journeyed straight to Utah.

When the California gold rush of 1849 started, Kanesville saw a dramatic increase in population, but not due to fellow Mormons. The 49ers who came to town on their way west were a rougher bunch. Soon saloons sprang up on the outskirts of Kanesville.

Hyde, who was still the leader of the Mormons at Kanesville, used his newspaper as a way to fight the sin he saw around him. He wrote story after story about the evils of saloons, gambling, and holding horse races on Sundays. Tensions between the Kanesville Mormons and the 49ers became heated.

In 1852, Hyde received word that the Mormon settlement in Utah was ready. He was ordered to bring the Kanesville Mormons out west. By now there were more than twelve thousand Mormons living in Kanesville. Not all of them traveled west with Hyde, but most did.

By 1853, the Mormon's Grand Encampment was all but deserted. The other residents of Kanesville petitioned the Iowa Legislature to allow them to change the name of the community to something that didn't remind them of the Mormons. The legislature agreed and decided to recognize the spot as the place where Lewis and Clark had first met with Indians on their expedition fifty years before. The new name of Kanesville was Council Bluffs.

All in all, nearly seventy thousand Mormons traveled at least part of the Mormon Trail, which officially runs from Illinois to Utah. A good majority of them came through Iowa, and some decided to settle in the Hawkeye State.

THE TABOR
UNDERGROUND RAILROAD

1857

The sun was setting behind the trees on the west side of Tabor when John Todd stepped out of his house. It was early December in 1857. Todd held a lantern in one hand. After pulling the door shut behind him, Todd stuck his other hand in his pocket to keep it warm and stepped off the low front porch. He glanced up and down the street in front of his house and then casually walked around to the back of the house. Crossing the frozen ground, Todd reached his barn and slipped inside.

"Who's there?" a rough voice whispered in the darkness.

Todd set the lantern on a small crate and adjusted the flame. Its light fell on the lined and weary face of his old friend, John Brown. Todd smiled.

Brown rose and came toward Todd. The men shook hands.

"Are they gone?" Brown asked.

"Yes," Todd replied, "and I don't think they will be back anytime soon."

Brown and Todd were discussing the sudden arrival of a posse from Missouri. They had traced a group of runaway slaves to the town of Tabor and had ridden in that afternoon on steaming horses. The townspeople of Tabor denied knowledge of any such runaways being in their area, and it seemed as though the posse believed them. They had ridden out several hours before.

Brown turned and whistled sharply into the dark barn. After a moment, Todd could see movement, and then a group of about a dozen black men and women materialized out of the darkness. They stared mutely at Todd.

"Brothers and sisters," Todd began in his strong, commanding voice, "please do not be afraid. Captain Brown here has brought you to a safe place. You can stay for a few days and then head east to Des Moines and on north to Canada."

Todd could sense the tension leave the group. They had been on the run for weeks, first fleeing Missouri for Kansas to the west, then turning north into Nebraska, then crossing the Missouri River back east into Iowa. They were finally in a free state, but still had a long road ahead of them.

"Let's head into the house and get you some supper," Todd said, swinging open the barn door.

Brown led the way to Todd's house. He was familiar with the property, having spent much time in and around Tabor in recent years. As the runaway slaves went inside the house, Brown held up a hand to prevent Todd from joining them. The two men faced each other in the yard as the first stars appeared in the night sky.

"I am here for more than just bringing these men and women through," Brown began. "I have come to collect the Bibles I left here."

Todd nodded. He had several crates in his dugout basement that were labeled "Beecher's Bibles." It made sense for Todd, a Congregational Church minister, to keep extra Bibles around, but anyone who opened those crates was in for a surprise. They did not contain Bibles, but instead were filled with Sharps rifles. The "Beecher's" label was in honor of another abolitionist, Rev. Henry Ward Beecher, brother to Harriet Beecher Stowe, who had authored *Uncle Tom's Cabin* several years before.

"I do have the Bibles as well as two cannons and shells," Todd replied, nodding in the direction of the barn.

"Good," said Brown. "I'm going to take them with me when I leave and have them shipped to a farm I know of in Maryland."

"Is that where they are needed?" asked Todd.

Brown grunted. "No, but it's close to a place I know called Harper's Ferry. They have an armory there that might just give me what I need."

Todd and Brown turned and headed inside.

Rev. John Todd was one of the founders of Tabor. He and a group of settlers had arrived in the area in the early 1850s. Most of them were people Todd had known for a long time, as they had all been students together at Oberlin College in Oberlin, Ohio. Oberlin College was a religious school with a commitment to progressive causes, including the eradication of slavery in the United States. The college, like Ohio itself, was saturated with Underground Railroad stops, where escaped slaves could find help as they sought freedom in the north.

Todd and his friends brought that mindset with them when they settled in western Iowa. Almost immediately, Tabor became involved in the Underground Railroad. That involvement only increased in 1855 when abolitionist John Brown made his first visit to Tabor. Brown was soon making regular stops in Tabor, and even used the area as a field hospital for some of his men who were injured in a fight in Kansas.

Todd often spoke to his congregation on the evils of slavery. His strong tone and logical mind gave Tabor residents the courage to open their homes and outbuildings to escaped slaves. Even though

Iowa was a free state, her citizens could still be fined or receive jail time for helping slaves escape. Every so often a posse from Missouri would ride into Tabor looking for runaways. Many Tabor residents had hiding places in attics and basements of their homes, and even under false bottoms in their wagons.

The residents of Tabor were accommodating of John Brown; although they were pious, they were not pacifist. When Brown set up a camp in Tabor to train some of his "soldiers," the citizens of Tabor did what they could to help. They allowed Brown's soldiers to park their wagons, erect their tents, and stockpile ammunition in the public square. The western part of Iowa was very sparsely settled during this time, and the Tabor citizens were not afraid of a sudden raid.

However, in December 1858, a year after Brown had removed his stash of rifles and cannons from the Todd property, the town of Tabor came to a crossroads regarding their involvement with the abolitionist. That December, Brown raided three plantations in Missouri to liberate the slaves who were on the properties. In the chaos, the plantations were plundered and a plantation owner was killed. Brown, his men, and twelve slaves, including a newborn, fled into Kansas and then Nebraska. They arrived in Tabor in February 1859.

When Brown arrived in Tabor, his good friend John Todd was away. The townsfolk of Tabor hid Brown and the slaves in the local schoolhouse, but their attitude changed when they heard reports of the devastation and murder committed by Brown and his men in Missouri. After much discussion, the Tabor city fathers crafted a resolution regarding John Brown. It read: ". . . while we sympathize with the oppressed, and will do all that we conscientiously can to help them in their efforts for freedom; nevertheless, we have no sympathy with those who go to Slave States to entice away slaves and take property or life when necessary to attain that end."

Brown was bitterly disappointed in Tabor's reaction and soon left with his men and the escaped slaves. He returned to Tabor only once more, that following September, one month before he was captured and killed after the failed raid at Harper's Ferry.

The Civil War soon consumed the nation. John Todd left Tabor again, this time to volunteer as a chaplain in the Union Army. He was assigned to the 46th Iowa Infantry. After one hundred days of service, Todd was mustered out and returned to Tabor.

Todd continued to advance his ideas of equality and integration. In 1866, he helped grow the Tabor Literary Institute into Tabor College, which was open to males and females of all races and all walks of life. Although Todd passed away in 1894 and Tabor College closed in 1927, John Todd is remembered for his vision of an egalitarian society on the Iowa prairie.

LITTLE BROWN CHURCH
IN THE VALE

1857

It was late in the day when the stagecoach carrying William Pitts made a stop in Bradford, Iowa. Looking out from his coach, Pitts saw a picturesque community nestled amid a thick forest near the Cedar River.

Pitts asked the stagecoach driver how long they would be staying in Bradford. Assured that he would have enough time to stretch his legs, the music teacher from Wisconsin stepped down from the coach and started off along Cedar Street.

Bradford was located in the southwest corner of Chickasaw County, about thirty-five miles north of Cedar Falls. Pitts was just passing through; he was on his way to visit his fiancé, and the stagecoach route from his home in southern Wisconsin took him through this part of Iowa.

It was June 1857, and Bradford had all the signs of an up-and-coming community. The town was less than ten years old, but it boasted a population of more than five hundred people, a hotel, and a mill, and there was even talk of a railroad being built through town. Pitts nodded thoughtfully. Yes, traveling by railroad would be much more convenient and relaxing than his current mode of transportation.

Pitts turned and looked back at the stagecoach. They had stopped in Bradford to change out the horses. So far, the tired and drooping team that had brought them this far had yet to be unyoked. The stagecoach driver was visiting with a few of Bradford's townspeople, most likely sharing the latest news.

Pitts figured he had a bit more time to wander. As he strolled down Cedar Street, the late afternoon sun broke out from behind a cloud. Pitts stopped and surveyed the scene in front of him in awe.

Before him lay a lush, green vale. The land sloped gently to the west and was ringed with trees. At the far end, Pitts could see a glint of sunlight reflecting off the Cedar River. The loveliness of the scene moved him. In his mind, Pitts could easily imagine a simple country church situated in the vale, its doors opened wide and its bells gaily ringing.

Pitts didn't know how long he stood gazing at the spot, but he soon heard the voice of the stagecoach driver calling and shook himself into the present. With one last look at the valley, Pitts slowly turned and headed back up the road.

As the stagecoach continued on its journey, Pitts found his mind returning to that lovely scene near Bradford. Once he was finally back in Wisconsin, he decided to put his feelings down on paper.

By the light of his lantern, Pitts began writing: "There's a church in the valley by the wildwood, no lovelier spot in the dale; no place is so dear to my childhood as the little brown church in the vale . . ."

As Pitts continued writing, what emerged from his pen was a poem that he eventually called "The Church in the Wildwood." Pitts wrote several verses, then used his musical ability to craft a simple, lilting tune in common time to match the poem. Satisfied with his interpretation of the scene and what it inspired in him, Pitts set the music in a desk drawer and went on with his life.

Meanwhile, back in Bradford, the spiritual leaders of the community decided the time was right for them to build a Congregational Church to serve the town. One of the families in town owned a large empty lot in a vale near the Cedar River. They donated it as a building site for the new church. Another family volunteered to quarry limestone for the foundation, and yet another family donated timber for the structure. The foundation was laid in 1860 and, over the next few years, the church slowly went up.

It was a simple structure, with the main space dedicated as a sanctuary. Three pointed-arch windows lined either side of the church, which was fronted by a tall bell tower. While the citizens of Bradford were pleased with their new place of worship, they were less than enthused by the color. To save money, church leaders had settled for the cheapest paint they could find. That paint was Ohio Mineral Paint, and it only came in one color: brown.

As the church was nearing completion, Bradford also began planning for a new school called the Bradford Academy. The school would provide advanced education to Bradford's youth and focus on the arts, including music. Teachers were hired from near and far, including one music teacher named William Pitts of Fredericksburg, Iowa, formerly of Wisconsin.

Pitts had married his fiancé and moved to Fredericksburg to be near her family. He remembered Bradford as the inspiration for his song "The Church in the Wildwood," which he still had packed away somewhere. Imagine Pitts's surprise when he arrived in Bradford and found a little brown church in the vale, right where he dreamed it should be!

Pitts dug out his composition and taught it to his class at the Bradford Academy. During the official dedication of the church,

Pitts's song was the featured part of the program. Young voices raised in song filled the church: "Oh, come, come, come, come, come to the church in the wildwood, oh, come to the church in the dale. No spot is so dear to my childhood as the little brown church in the vale."

That was the peak for Bradford. The railroad never came, and the community began to shrink. The Bradford Academy closed in 1877 and the church followed suit in 1888. Bradford became unincorporated.

Not all was lost, though. Around 1914 the Society for the Preservation of the Little Brown Church was created, and regular services began again. "The Church in the Wildwood" song was becoming popular once more, thanks to the Weatherwax Brothers Quartet from Charles City, Iowa.

Between 1910 and 1921 the Weatherwax Brothers Quartet toured the United States and Canada, specializing in gospel singing. Their chosen theme song was none other than "The Church in the Wildwood." Thousands of people in the United States and Canada became familiar with the tune.

Pitts's music career ended soon after his time at the Bradford Academy. Putting aside music for a more practical career in medicine, Pitts moved to Chicago in 1865 to attend Rush Medical College. To pay his enrollment fee, Pitts sold the rights to "The Church in the Wildwood" to a Chicago music publisher for $25.

Today, the town of Bradford in Chickasaw County is no more. The church, though, remains popular, especially as a wedding destination. Thousands of weddings are held there each year, and there is even an annual wedding reunion in August for all the couples who have said their nuptials there. Regular Sunday services are still held in the church, where the closing benediction each week is "The Church in the Wildwood."

THE CIRCUS COMES TO TOWN

1867

At the end of one particularly long, hot summer day in McGregor, Iowa, in 1867, brothers Al, Gus, Otto, Alf, and Charles turned their backs on the Mississippi River and raced home. As they headed up Main Street, Al, Gus, and Otto, the three older boys, each kept an eye over their shoulder on Alf and Charles, the babies. Finally all five boys reached their home on Walton Street.

Their parents, August and Salome Marie, were waiting, along with one-year-old John. After the excitement of the day, the boys could hardly wait to tell their parents of their idea. Al, who at age fourteen was the oldest, had been selected by his brothers to talk first.

"Mother, Father," Al started, nodding at each in turn. Before he could continue, thirteen-year-old Gus broke in.

"We want to start a circus!" Gus exclaimed.

August and Salome Ringling exchanged a look. They knew this was coming. It all started last summer when three steamboat circuses stopped off at the McGregor riverboat landing on their journey between St. Paul to the north and New Orleans way down south. This summer, four circuses had come to town—one complete with an elephant! August and Salome had let the boys go down to the landing at the end of Main Street to watch the circus folk unload their tents and animals, set everything up, and prepare for the evening show. Whenever August needed help in his shop or Salome needed a hand at home, they knew they only had to look around at the circus to find any of the Ringling boys.

Otto had taken over the sales pitch from Gus.

"It will be the greatest show on earth," he piped up, trying to make his nine-year-old voice sound much older.

As the sun set on the Ringling home in McGregor that summer night, the brothers inside the house were busy planning their new venture.

The Ringlings had lived in McGregor since 1860. August came to the United States from Hanover, Germany, when he was twenty-two years old. His original surname had been Rungeling, but as August learned English, he decided to Americanize his name by changing it to Ringling.

August worked as a harness maker. He married Salome Marie Juliar in February 1852, and in December of that year, the two welcomed their first son, Al. Al was born in Chicago and was followed less than two years later by Gus, born in July 1854 in Milwaukee. By June 1858 the family was in Baraboo, Wisconsin, where they welcomed Otto into the world. Alf was the first son born in McGregor in 1863 and was followed by Charles in 1864. John was born in 1866 and Henry, the seventh son, joined the family in 1868.

After two summers of observing the ins and outs of putting on a circus, the Ringling Brothers were ready to organize their own. With the blessing of their parents, they erected a makeshift tent in their backyard on Walton Street and opened their own circus. It ran only on Saturdays, and admission started out at ten straight pins.

The brothers soon started charging a one-cent admission to cover their expenses. The circus's main feature, an exotic animal, needed to be fed. Of course, the exotic animal was only the old white horse that belonged to the next-door neighbor, but that wasn't the only animal they featured. They also had dogs, rabbits, a bullfrog, and kittens billed as being from Timbuctoo.

The Ringling Brothers worked very hard to re-create what they had learned from the steamboat circuses. They kept the animals outside and put on main acts inside the barn. The main acts included swings, daring walks across a long beam, and acrobatics. They started having a parade up Main Street to their barn to help promote the circus.

In 1872, the Ringling family moved across the river from McGregor to Prairie du Chien, Wisconsin. The brothers kept putting on circuses while they finished school. In 1874, their baby sister, Ida, was born. By the early 1880s the Ringling Brothers had gained regional fame as providers of entertainment and were charging admission rates of fifty cents for adults and twenty-five cents for children.

By 1888 they were billing themselves as the "Ringling Brothers United Monster Shows, Great Double Circus, Royal European Menagerie, Museum, Caravan, and Congress of Trained Animals." A year later, in 1889, the Ringling Brothers were financially able to use the railroad as a source of transportation and became the first circus to travel the country coast to coast.

The Ringling Brothers circus spent more than $400,000 in 1907 to buy out the Barnum & Bailey show, their main competitor. In 1929, they spent $2 million to purchase the American Circus Co., becoming the number one provider of circuses in America.

The Great Depression of the 1930s and technological advancements in the mid-1900s caused the decline of audiences for the Ringling Bros. and Barnum & Bailey Circus. The last Ringling, a nephew to the original brothers, sold the business in the 1960s. It still toured with the Ringling name and continued to be billed as "The Greatest Show on Earth" until May 2017, when a further drop in ticket sales led to its final act. People for the Ethical Treatment of Animals (PETA) took credit for the demise of the circus, citing their success in pressuring Ringling Brothers to remove wild animals from their acts. The exclusion of elephants from the circus in 2016 is considered the primary cause of the show's ultimate failure.

BIRTHPLACE OF A PRESIDENT

1874

At the tender age of eleven, Herbert Hoover knew far too much about death.

The year before, in 1884, the West Branch, Iowa, lad had lost his mother, Hulda. Only five years previous, in 1880, Hoover had watched as his father was buried. Now he was about to be separated from his sister and brother and sent to Oregon to live with family he didn't even know.

As young Herbert packed one suitcase with all his belongings in preparation for his journey to Oregon, he thought about his childhood. He had been born in a two-room cottage in West Branch on August 10, 1874. His parents were hard-working Quakers who had originally come to the West Branch area in covered wagons. Dad Jesse was a blacksmith and mom Hulda was a Quaker minister.

As Quakers, the Hoovers taught their son the value of simplicity, integrity, equality, peace, and service. Herbert had attended school at the Quaker Friends Meetinghouse and then the West

Branch school; even after his father died, Herbert's mother insisted he continue with his schooling.

After Hulda died of pneumonia, Herbert spent some time with his paternal uncle and aunt, Allen and Millie Hoover. Now, however, he was going to leave his sister, Mary, and brother, Theodore, in Iowa and go live with his maternal uncle and aunt, John and Laura Minthorn.

Herbert Hoover arrived in Oregon a solemn boy. The Minthorns accepted him into their home, but they were very different parents than Jesse and Hulda had been. They were strict and offered little comfort to the lonely boy from Iowa.

Hoover later defined that time in his life as character-building. He attended the Friends Pacific Academy in Oregon, and, although he did not do well academically, he was able to secure entrance into the newly opened Stanford University in Palo Alto, California.

Hoover studied mining at Stanford, using his summer vacations to volunteer on US geological surveys throughout the western portion of the country. At the age of twenty-three, Hoover began a job as an engineer in Australia, opening new gold mines. In 1899, he married his college sweetheart, Lou Henry, who had also been born in Iowa, and the two left for China. Hoover had received a promotion and was named as the chief engineer for the Chinese Bureau of Mines.

By the time World War I broke out in Europe in 1914, the Hoovers and their two sons, ten-year-old Herbert Jr. and seven-year-old Allan, were living in London. Hoover was working as an independent mining consultant. His mother's lessons on service were put to use as Hoover, who by now was very wealthy, loaned money to stranded Americans to help them get home. Hoover stayed in London and soon earned the nickname "The Great Humanitarian" for his work in establishing the Commission for Relief in Belgium during the war.

The Hoovers soon returned to America, and, in 1917, Herbert was named by President Woodrow Wilson as the US Food Administrator. He created the American Relief Commission to help provide food to Europe after World War I and by 1921 was the US Secretary of Commerce.

In 1928, Herbert Hoover ran as a Republican candidate to become the thirty-first president of the United States and won by an overwhelming majority.

Hoover was a big man; at his inauguration he was 5 feet 11 inches tall and weighed 210 pounds. Dr. Joel T. Boone, Hoover's personal physician, encouraged his patient to exercise more and even invented a game for Hoover to play. Called "Hoover-Ball" by a *New York Times* reporter, the game featured two teams of two to four players on either side of an eight-foot-high net on a court that was sixty-six feet by thirty feet. The two teams threw a six-pound medicine ball back and forth across the net. Scores were tallied just like in a tennis match.

Hoover enjoyed the game so much that he invited, or perhaps insisted, that his Cabinet and other high-ranking government officials play with him. Every morning, except for Sunday, Hoover and his Cabinet would play a round or two of Hoover-Ball. If the weather was especially bad, they retreated to the basement of the White House to play. The press had a field day with the arrangement, calling the group the "Medicine Ball Cabinet."

Hoover dropped the extra pounds and ended his one and only term as president at 185 pounds. He spent his years after his presidency serving on various commissions and writing. Hoover died in 1964 and was buried in West Branch.

Today, West Branch celebrates Hoover's Hometown Days every August. In addition to a parade and live music, the big draw of the festivities is the Hoover-Ball national championship tournament.

Herbert Hoover took the lessons he learned as a young Quaker boy on the Iowa prairie with him throughout the world. When he learned that he had secured the presidential nomination in 1928, he wrote, "My country owes me no debt. It gave me, as it gives every boy and girl, a chance. It gave me schooling, independence of action, opportunity for service and honor. In no other land could a boy from a country village, without inheritance or influential friends, look forward with unbounded hope. My whole life has taught me what America means. I am indebted to my country beyond any human power to repay."

ESTHERVILLE METEORITE

At breakfast on the morning of May 10, 1879, the most exciting news found in Estherville's newspaper was the short item about milk being sold in glass bottles in some of the big cities on the East Coast. The more than seven hundred residents of Estherville chuckled at the thought of such a luxury.

Estherville, located in Emmet County in north-central Iowa, was like many small villages on the plains during that time period. The community had been platted and settled in the late 1850s and boasted a post office, a mill that ground corn and wheat, a bank, and a weekly newspaper called the *Northern Vindicator*.

Early settlers traded in their ox-drawn wagons for log cabins, then wood-framed houses, then stone and brick abodes. Residents gathered at the schoolhouse or in the public square, and most of the talk around town was whether or not the community should become incorporated.

After May 10, 1879, the talk of the town was the fireball that lit up the sky.

It started out as a pinprick of light, brighter than any star, to the southwest. Gradually, then with increasing speed, the light grew in intensity and size traveling northeast. Citizens of Estherville and those who lived as far as fifteen miles away gaped in awe at the fireball above them. It was a meteorite! A long trail of dust and flames split the sky behind the fireball.

As the meteorite came closer, the earth shook. Books fell off shelves, crockery rattled in cupboards, windows broke.

Just before impact, the meteor split into three distinct parts. The three pieces crashed into the fertile Iowa soil, and a shower of smaller pieces, from the size of a pea to the size of a dinner plate, rained down from the sky. Dust filled the air.

The residents of Estherville immediately went in search of the three largest sections of the meteorite. The largest piece, which at 27 inches by 22.75 inches by 15 inches and weighing 431 pounds, was found in a six-foot-deep crater on the Sever Lee farm just over two miles north of Estherville and required the services of a well digger to remove it from the ground.

The meteorite was dark gray in color with flashes of metallic silver. Scientists were called to Estherville to examine it and found it to be of the rare mesosiderite class, meteorites containing iron, nickel, and sulphur, which make up less than 2 percent of known asteroids.

Controversy over the ownership of the meteorite ensued. Sever Lee had defaulted on payments for his property and didn't own the land on which he farmed. The well digger was actually hired by some local boys. The boys loaded the meteorite onto a wagon and started on their way to Chicago to display it—and perhaps sell it to the highest bidder! Word reached the boys that they were instructed to return the meteorite, so they turned around and headed home.

Meanwhile, a lawyer from Keokuk heard about the meteorite and researched the land where it was found. Learning that Sever Lee had defaulted on payment on the farm, the lawyer purchased Lee's land out from under him and sought a writ of attachment for the meteorite. The lawyer soon sold the meteorite to the British Museum.

On May 14, 1879, just four days after the meteor fell to earth, the second section was found on the A. A. Pingrey farm just west of the Lee farm. The second piece was smaller, weighing 151 pounds. It was found four and a half feet below the surface of the ground. Apparently unaware of the value of the meteorite, Pingrey gave it away to his neighbor, John Homer. Homer immediately hid the meteorite in case Pingrey changed his mind, and soon thereafter sold it to the University of Minnesota.

The third fragment of the original meteorite was not discovered for another eleven years. In February 1890, the Pietz brothers were trapping in an area southwest of Estherville when they came across a 106-pound meteorite buried five feet into the ground. By that time, meteorite gathering had become a popular family activity. Thousands of pieces of the meteorite were displayed in homes around the area, made into jewelry, or, if big enough, sold to various museums, including the Smithsonian in Washington, DC, and natural history museums in Chicago, Vienna, Munich, and Paris.

Only about two hundred mesosiderites have been found in the entire world. The total weight of the Estherville Meteorite when all the pieces are added together equals nearly 750 pounds, making it one of the largest recorded meteorites to have fallen on North America. A piece of it resides at the Meteorite Center in Estherville.

KATE SHELLEY SAVES THE DAY

1881

Kate swallowed a sob as she reached forward with a trembling hand. The rain had plastered her nightgown to her body, and rivulets of water streamed down her face. Her hands were scratched and raw from grasping the boards as she crawled across the trestle. Her nightgown was torn in several places, and she had lost her lantern what seemed like hours ago.

A sudden flash of lightning illuminated the scene in front of Kate. The raging Des Moines River, swollen with rainwater, was fifty feet below her. The end of the bridge seemed miles away. And the rain kept coming down.

Kate gave very little thought to her own mortality; the fifteen-year-old was focused on getting across the Des Moines River Bridge and to the Moingona Station any way she could. If that meant crawling on her hands and knees the entire length of the bridge, then that's what she would do. Kate took a deep breath, steadied herself, and reached out her hand again.

Kate Shelley had been fitfully sleeping in the bed she shared with her mother and siblings in the small shack next to the Honey Creek Bridge near Boone. The heavy rains had started earlier in the day on July 6, 1881. By the time Kate and her family went to bed, the creek was rising. The sound of the rain and thunder kept Kate from falling deeper into sleep.

A loud, tearing crash jolted Kate upright in the bed. That was more than just thunder. Kate jumped out of bed and hurried to the window. A gasp escaped her lips as she viewed the scene before her.

"What is it, Kate?" asked her mother. She was sitting up in bed with her arms around Kate's siblings.

"The bridge—it's down! And the No. 12 is, too!" Kate exclaimed. The trestle that spanned Honey Creek had succumbed to the floodwaters and collapsed into the creek under the weight of the No. 12 train. Kate stared at the scene for a heartbeat more and then whirled to grab her late father's railroad jacket. She rushed to the fireplace and lit the family's only lantern.

"Kate," said her mother, "what are you doing?"

"I have to get to the Moingona Station and warn them," Kate replied as she tugged on her boots. "The Chicago Midnight Express hasn't gone over yet, but it will be coming soon. The train has to be stopped!"

One of Kate's siblings whimpered. As she absently stroked the child's back, Kate's mom took one last searching look at her oldest daughter. She knew it was futile to forbid Kate from going. Putting aside her terror, she simply whispered, "God be with you, Kate."

Kate smiled grimly at her mother before stepping outside into the rain. It was coming down in sheets, making it hard for Kate to see. She ran to the bank of Honey Creek and peered into the gloom. There, sticking out of the water under what was left of the Honey

Creek Bridge, was the No. 12 engine. Kate could see two men cling-ing to the branches of a tree at the edge of the creek.

Knowing she had no way of helping the men until the floodwa-ters went down, Kate turned her back on them and started off down the tracks. She would follow the tracks to the Moingona Station more than two and a half miles away and warn the stationmaster that the Honey Creek Bridge was out. The only thing standing in her way was the Des Moines River Bridge.

By the time Kate reached the Des Moines River Bridge, she was soaked and exhausted. Her feet and hands were numb. Kate swayed on her feet as she stared at the trestle in front of her. She hadn't stopped to think that the cross ties on the bridge were spaced nearly three feet apart to prevent pedestrians from using the bridge. But this was an emergency. How was she going to cross the bridge? She couldn't leap from one cross tie to another in this weather.

Kate's legs buckled and she fell to her knees. From that angle the 671 feet that she had to cross didn't look quite so intimidating. Kate tucked her nightgown around her legs and started forward, crawling from one cross tie to the next. The rain was still coming down, and now the wind started to blow.

After what seemed like hours, Kate reached solid ground. By sheer force of will, she got to her feet and continued down the track. She was lightheaded and wobbly, but knew she had to get from the bridge to the station as soon as she could.

Suddenly, the Moingona Station loomed in front of her. Kate feebly pushed at the door and stumbled into the warmth of the sta-tion when the door swung open. She swayed on her feet, blinking at the alarmed faces swimming before her. She opened her mouth to tell them about the Honey Creek Bridge, and promptly collapsed in a dead faint.

Luckily, the stationmaster recognized Kate Shelley and knew where she lived. He rightly guessed what Kate had come to say and halted the two hundred-passenger Chicago Midnight Express just in time. Kate came out of her faint and insisted on leading a group of men to where the No. 12 engine had crashed when the Honey Creek Bridge gave way. The two men in the trees were rescued; two others perished.

Kate was recognized near and far as a hero, and accolades and gifts started pouring in. She was given free tuition at Simpson College, which she attended for one year. She soon returned to Boone County and taught school for several years. In 1903, Kate was named as the stationmaster at Moingona.

In 1901, a new steel-beam bridge was erected north of the previous Des Moines River Bridge. The new bridge was more than three times as high as the one Kate had crossed and was the longest and highest double-track railroad bridge in the world.

Kate Shelley stayed in Boone County the rest of her life and worked as the Moingona stationmaster until 1910. She died in 1912.

The new Des Moines River Bridge was named the Kate Shelley High Bridge and retains that name today. The Moingona Station is now a museum and features the incredible story of one courageous Iowa girl.

FENELON PLACE ELEVATOR

1882

Julius K. Graves had lived in Dubuque for twenty-seven years before he implemented his grand idea. For most of those twenty-seven years, Graves traveled via horse and buggy from his home at 25 Fenelon Street in the bluffs to his work in downtown Dubuque. Even though it was a distance of only two and a half blocks, navigating the steep bluff was impossible for the horse and buggy. Instead, Graves had to endure a lengthy trip around the back of the bluff and up and down gently sloping roads and switchbacks during his commute. The longer route meant it took Graves thirty minutes to get to work and thirty minutes to get home every day.

The long commute time also meant that Graves did not have time for a nap when he went home for lunch.

In 1882, Graves decided to do something about his commute. He vowed to tunnel into the bottom of the bluff and install a gas-powered elevator that would lift him to his four-acre property on the top of the hill. It was a daring idea for the late 1800s, but Graves knew he was the man to do it.

A banker by trade, Graves had arrived in Dubuque in 1855. By 1858 he owned the J.K. Graves & Company Bank, which later merged with the State Bank of Iowa. Graves served as vice president and general manager. During his long career in Dubuque, he was also president and major stockholder of the Key City Gas Company.

Politically, Graves served as Dubuque's mayor in the late 1860s before being elected to the Iowa state legislature in 1876. In 1881, Graves was elected as an Iowa state senator.

Graves's real interest, however, was trains. At different points in his life, Graves was president of the Dubuque Street Railway Company, the Chicago, Dubuque, and Minnesota Railroad, the Chicago, Clinton, and Dubuque Railroad, and the Iowa Pacific. Using his knowledge of railroads, and inspired by incline rails he had seen in Europe, Graves decided to scrap the vertical elevator shaft and instead build a short railroad to go up the side of the hill.

Graves received permission from the Dubuque City Council to go ahead with construction of the elevator/railroad in June 1882, and one month later it was ready to be used.

On July 25, 1882, Graves climbed into the Swiss-style railcar at the end of his street on the top of the 189-foot bluff. The open car had been designed and built by a local engineer named John Bell. Another local, Clifton Trewin, designed the contraption used to lift and lower the car along the 296-foot line, incorporating hemp ropes, a coal-fired steam engine boiler, and a winch. Very slowly, Graves rode to the bottom of the bluff and disembarked from the car onto Fourth Street in downtown Dubuque.

The Fenelon Place Elevator was up and running! It quickly became the talk of the town. Dubuque residents, and others from throughout Iowa and the Midwest, came to watch the railcar traverse up and down the bluff, navigating an incline that was 74 degrees in some places.

Due to friction with the hemp rope, the elevator caught fire occasionally. After a particularly bad fire on July 9, 1886, which destroyed the elevator, Graves recouped his investment by rebuilding the elevator and opening it up to the public for five cents a ride.

In 1893, after another fire destroyed the elevator again, ten of Graves's neighbors, who had gotten used to riding the elevator to and from downtown Dubuque, each invested $250 to form the Fenelon Place Elevator Company. The company invested in a steel cable to replace the hemp rope, and added a third rail. That third rail, along with a fourth rail at a bulge in the middle of the line, allowed two cars to pass each other on the route. A twenty-five-horsepower electric motor replaced the original gas-powered one.

Graves passed away in 1898, but the elevator kept running. In 1916, the wooden railcars were replaced with steel-constructed cars. Passengers could still ride the elevator for five cents; the fare remained a nickel until 1962. That year, the cost went up to ten cents a ride.

Throughout the twentieth century, upgrades were made as needed, including a new gearbox. In 1978, the Fenelon Place Elevator was named to the National Register of Historic Places. It is one of the steepest and shortest railroads in the world. Passengers can still ride it today; fares are $1.50 one-way for adults and 75 cents for kids. What started as a way to save time and energy for an 1880s Dubuque businessman has turned into an Iowa tourist destination.

BELLE PLAINE GEYSER

1886

On August 26, 1886, Belle Plaine splashed onto the Iowa map in dramatic fashion.

Located between Des Moines and Cedar Rapids, Belle Plaine was a growing community, thanks to the Union Pacific Railroad. New neighborhoods were platted and settled every year; between 1880 and 1890 the population of Belle Plaine increased by one thousand people.

In 1886, William Weir of Monticello, Iowa, was hired for $175 to drill a well at the intersection of Beach and Washington Streets in Belle Plaine. While several wells had already been dug in Belle Plaine in recent months for business purposes, this well was to be for fire suppression.

Weir was a stonemason by trade and had only recently started digging wells. He began by drilling a two-inch opening for the well. Water started shooting out of the bore, and Weir and his sons stepped back to wait for the flow to ebb. To Weir's surprise and shock, instead of slowing down, the water pressure seemed to increase. Slowly but surely, the two-inch-diameter bore was widening, first to three inches in diameter, then six inches, then twelve inches. Weir and his sons tried everything they could to cap the well, but to no avail. Finally, after measuring the opening of the bore at more than three feet wide, Weir and his sons packed up all their gear and fled.

The citizens of Belle Plaine optimistically waited for the Weirs to return, but as the days went by with no word, they realized it would be up to them to fix the problem. And quite the problem it was: The geyser was shooting out water fifty-three feet into the air, and an estimated five million gallons of water was lost daily during those first few days. The water collected to form a pond at the intersection, and the streets all around the geyser flooded.

Soon the geyser, nicknamed "Jumbo," settled down to a mere five-foot-high fountain. Water wasn't the only thing gushing out the ground; later, Belle Plaine residents recalled the tons of sand, rocks, wood, and even bones that washed out of the earth.

At first, the city enjoyed its new claim to fame, welcoming tourists from far and wide to see what was called the "8th Wonder of the World."

People also came from far and wide to attempt to cap the well. Finally, on October 6, 1887, fourteen long months after the geyser had erupted, the local Palmer Brothers Foundry found a way to shut it down. It took three hundred feet of pipe, forty carloads of stone, and 130 barrels of cement.

At some point the streets of Belle Plaine were renamed. The intersection of Beach and Washington is now the intersection of 8th Street and 8th Avenue, and a granite marker stands as a reminder of the Belle Plaine geyser.

MUSCATINE PEARL
BUTTON FACTORY

1891

John Boepple was having a difficult time settling into Muscatine, Iowa. It was 1891 and the German immigrant had arrived in the United States earlier in the year with grand ideas of a new business venture. Boepple was looking for shells.

Boepple came from a long line of button makers. Back in Germany, Boepple had been one of the first button makers to switch from animal horns to shell to make his buttons. Shells were much cheaper to obtain. He had been shipping in loads of shells from the United States to his shop in Germany, but the taxes were getting higher. Boepple decided to relocate to America and get the shells straight from the source.

Boepple soon realized that it was too expensive to get ocean shells for his buttons, even though he was in the United States and no longer had to pay international tariffs. He started searching for freshwater mussels in the Mississippi River, which formed the eastern border of Muscatine, thinking that the tough, thick mussel shells would be perfect for buttons. He found an abundant supply in the river, but lacked the money to harvest them.

Boepple finally found a financial partner in William Molis of Muscatine. The two opened the world's first freshwater pearl button plant in 1891 and almost singlehandedly turned Muscatine into the "Pearl Button Capital of the World" overnight.

From 1891 to the 1940s, Muscatine produced more than 1.5 billion buttons each year, totaling 40 percent of the world's supply. Boepple and Molis's factory was soon joined by approximately forty others, all up and down the Mississippi River. From harvesting the shells to cleaning them to drilling out circular buttons to polishing them, button-making soon became the area's largest industry, employing half the local workforce.

Clammers were the first line in producing buttons. A clammer was a fisherman who specialized in finding good mussels. Camps of clammers could be found up and down the riverbanks; while the men harvested the shell beds, the women and children would steam open the mussels and ready them for the next step in the process.

After soaking for about a week to soften them, the shells were taken to various locations to be cut into buttons. Some of the best cutting shops were located in family homes, where each member of the family had a job. Someone had to hold the shell in place with tongs while another person wielded the circular drill to cut out the button-to-be. The circles were then collected and sold to a factory.

The factories employed machinery like the Barry Double Automatic, a contraption invented by the Barry family of Muscatine that would drill perfectly circular button holes, either in pairs of two or groups of four. The use of the machine and standardization of the process increased production, allowing for more than twenty thousand buttons to be made daily at most factories.

The final step in making a pearl button was polishing. A pumice stone helped smooth the edges of the button, and then the buttons were tossed in a steam barrel with a variety of acids to give the buttons some shine.

Once the pearl buttons were ready to be sold, another group of workers was responsible for sorting and displaying the buttons. Women and girls would sew the buttons onto colorful cards that the button factory used to market their goods.

The by-product of the button-making business was also good for Muscatine. Leftover shell chips were often used as fill when paving alleys and streets around town. Local farmers would collect chips and shell dust to use as a natural insecticide. Mussel shells deemed unworthy to be used for buttons were turned into fishing lures, jewelry, and even belt buckles.

The making of pearl buttons was a fairly short-lived enterprise. Production peaked in 1916, but the mussel beds around Muscatine were soon depleted, and clammers had to travel up and down the river to more than a dozen states to find the shells. Factories began closing in the 1940s as the invention of plastic, a cheap and moldable material, made the pearl button obsolete. By the 1960s the few button companies still in production in Muscatine had switched over to plastic.

For just over fifty years, pearl buttons were found everywhere in the world, and the majority of those buttons were made in Muscatine factories. For that brief time, Muscatine really was the Pearl Button Capital of the World.

GROWING RED DELICIOUS

1893

Jesse Hiatt placed the rough crate on the workbench just inside his barn. He headed deeper into the barn for an armful of hay to use as cushioning. Returning to the workbench, Hiatt lined the bottom of the crate with hay and then carefully set a peck of oddly shaped apples in the crate, nestling them down deep for good measure. Hiatt stuffed the excess hay around the apples. Before adding the last layer of hay on top, Hiatt slipped in a note with his name and the name he had given this apple variety: Hawkeye.

Hiatt set the lid on the crate and carefully hammered it into place. The Hawkeye was not the only apple Hiatt had created; he was also fond of his Hiatt Sweet and Hiatt Black apples. However, he was putting his faith in his Hawkeye apple, anticipating that the sweet flavor and scent of the red- and yellow-striped apple would win first prize at the 1893 International New Fruit Show sponsored by Stark Bro's Nurseries and Orchards in Louisiana, Missouri.

In the beginning, Hiatt had had a love-hate relationship with his Hawkeye apple. He first noticed the volunteer seedling growing in his acreage of Yellow Bellflower apples more than twenty years before and tried—twice!—to cut it down. When the tree returned the third time, Hiatt shrugged and let it grow. The fruit it bore was oblong in shape and had five large bumps on the bottom. Hiatt tried to sell his new apple, which he had named Hawkeye, to local nurserymen, but was told the shape of the apple was too odd. Hiatt shrugged again and resigned himself to enjoying the fruit alone.

In the meantime, Stark Bro's Nurseries and Orchards was on the hunt for the best apple in the nation. Stark Bro's president, Clarence Stark, wanted to find an apple to take the place of the then-popular Ben Davis apple. The Ben Davis grew anywhere, didn't bruise, and was very hardy; however, it had one big drawback: It didn't taste very good.

Stark Bro's decided to have a contest. They sent thousands of invitations to apple growers all over the country, asking for entries in its first International New Fruit Show. They received hundreds of entries from twenty-seven different states, including one from Jesse Hiatt of Peru, Iowa.

After Hiatt shipped off his peck of Hawkeye apples, life returned to normal. The months went by with no word from the International New Fruit Show, and Hiatt assumed his apple didn't make the cut.

Life, however, was not normal at Stark Bro's Nurseries and Orchards. The International New Fruit Show turned out to be a resounding success, mostly because of the discovery of what Clarence Stark called a "delicious" new apple. It was oblong in shape, had red and yellow stripes, and had five pronounced bumps on the bottom. It was perfect except for one detail: The show's organizers had misplaced the identification card and had no way of knowing who sent in the apple or where it came from.

Their solution was to replicate the 1893 International New Fruit Show and host the 1894 International New Fruit Show. Stark Bro's sent out invitations to the same list of growers they had used the previous year and asked for a repeat entry. Jesse Hiatt was one of those growers, so he packed up another peck of his Hawkeye apples and shipped it to the show.

This time, Stark Bro's Nurseries and Orchards wasted no time in declaring Jesse Hiatt's Hawkeye as the winner of the International New Fruit Show. Company representatives traveled to Peru and bought the sole rights to the fruit from Hiatt. They changed the name from Hawkeye to Stark Delicious.

Over the next twenty years, Stark Bro's spent hundreds of thousands of dollars marketing the apple throughout the country and eventually the world. In 1914, the Golden Delicious apple appeared, and the Stark Delicious was officially renamed Red Delicious.

Of the thousands of apple varieties in the world, Red Delicious remains one of the most recognized apples in America. And while new varieties are developed every year in nurseries and science labs, the Red Delicious takes pride in the fact that it is rooted in Iowa's history.

SUMMER OF DVOŘÁK

1893

With the majestic strains of his nearly completed *New World Symphony* playing in his head, Antonín Dvořák stepped out of the buggy onto the dusty street. The stocky composer felt himself relax as he looked around. His secretary was right: Spillville, Iowa, looked remarkably like his beloved Bohemia on the other side of the world. If there was any place in America that could help him recover from the stress of his job as director of the National Conservatory of Music in New York City, Spillville was it.

Dvořák turned back to the buggy and assisted his wife, Anna, down from her seat. The children and their housemaid, plus Anna's sister who had joined them for the summer, were already disembarking on the other side of the buggy. Dvořák's secretary, a man named Joseph J. Kovarik, was helping his father unhitch the horses from the buggy. The elder Kovarik, Johann, had picked up his son and the Dvořák clan from the train station five miles away in Calmar, Iowa, earlier that afternoon.

The famed Dvořák enjoyed his work at the National Conservatory of Music. The fifty-one-year-old had only been there one year, and this was his first summer off as stipulated in his contract. At the Conservatory, Dvořák used his days efficiently, which left him time to compose. Dvořák felt that being in America had inspired him to write perhaps his greatest accomplishment, the *New World Symphony*. He was looking forward to quiet moments in Iowa to put the finishing touches on the piece and focus on new compositions.

Even though Dvořák was artistically fulfilled, he was homesick for Bohemia. When Joseph Kovarik had announced he was going home to Spillville for the summer, Dvořák became intrigued. Kovarik often talked of Spillville and its 350 residents, the majority of them immigrants from Bohemia. The Czech culture was alive and well in Spillville.

Kovarik correctly read Dvořák's interest in Spillville and invited the composer to join him there for the summer of 1893. Dvořák didn't need much convincing, and on June 3, he and his family boarded a train for Iowa.

The ride west from New York was uneventful for the group. They watched the landscape fly by; Dvořák complained about the lack of beer on the train. After a short stop to sightsee in Chicago, the trip continued. They arrived in Iowa on June 5.

Dvořák and his family acclimated quickly to life in Spillville, Iowa. Dvořák would rise early and depart from the house he had rented for the summer. With opera glasses in one hand and a notebook in the other, he would head out on a long, meandering walk through Spillville and into the surrounding countryside. One of his favorite places to walk was along the Turkey River, on the eastern edge of town. Once near the river, he would take a break from his walk and use the opera glasses to bird watch. Dvořák's lilting *Humoresque*, composed the following year, was perhaps inspired by the birdsong he listened to every morning in Iowa. On the days he didn't take his opera glasses, Dvořák would carry a bucket of beer and simply enjoy the day.

After his early morning walk, Dvořák would attend Mass at Saint Wenceslaus Catholic Church. In very short order, Dvořák installed himself as the organist, playing at Mass all summer long, as well as for weddings and funerals.

Dvořák used the rest of his days for composing and socializing. He made fast friends with the local shoemaker and could be found most evenings in the town's tavern, visiting with Spillville residents about their shared Bohemian homeland.

However, no matter where he was, music was always on his mind. Dvořák took time that summer to compose for fun, for himself. If he didn't have his notebook with him, he would scribble snippets of music on his shirt cuff.

One of those snippets turned into the String Quartet No. 12 in F Major, Op. 96, nicknamed the "America Quartet." Dvořák, who wrote the piece in five days that summer, convinced his secretary Joseph, Joseph's father, and Joseph's sister to dust off their instruments and play it with him as soon as he completed it.

Dvořák's only complaint about Spillville that entire summer was the lack of certain amenities he was used to back in New York City. However, once he learned his cigar maker would ship cigars to him in Spillville, all was well again.

The composer turned fifty-two on September 8. Just over a week later, on September 16, the Dvořák family abruptly left Spillville amid rumors that the eldest daughter was planning to elope with a Spillville lad. While Dvořák repeatedly claimed to have the desire to return to Spillville permanently, he never walked those Iowa hills again.

Dvořák's time in Spillville was a gift not only to the composer but also to the immigrants who made up the town. His persona and genius made the Old World come alive again for the Bohemian transplants of this small Iowa community.

SNAKE ALLEY

1894

Located in the southeast corner of Iowa is a thriving river town by the name of Burlington. Established in the 1830s after the signing of the Black Hawk Treaty, Burlington experienced steady population growth in the early years; by 1890, more than twenty-two thousand people called Burlington home.

The original retail center of Burlington was platted along the Mississippi River, while the residential neighborhoods were built on the bluffs above. In 1894, in an effort to solve the tricky problem of transporting goods and people up the steep streets of Burlington, an experimental roadway was laid between Washington and Columbia Streets.

The road was built with two quarter turns and five half turns as it wound from Washington Street at the bottom to Columbia Street at the top. The serpentine look of the road gave it the name Snake Alley.

The switchback layout of Snake Alley meant that travelers going from Washington up to Columbia or Columbia down to Washington more than quadrupled their distance traveled. A straight-line reckoning measured the distance between the two streets at 58 feet. Taking the twisty Snake Alley equaled a distance of 275 feet!

The idea of Snake Alley came from the collective minds of three Burlington residents: Charles Starker, William Steyh, and George Kriechbaum. Starker had settled in Burlington in the mid-1800s because the land reminded him of his home in southern Germany. A trained architect and landscape engineer, he worked with city engineer Steyh and paving contractor Kriechbaum to develop Snake Alley based on vineyard paths commonly found in France and Germany.

Kriechbaum had perhaps the hardest job in constructing Snake Alley. Each locally fired blue-clay paving brick was laid individually on its side at a downward angle to provide better footing for horses. The slant switched from one curve to the next, with the high grade always to the outside. For his backbreaking work, Kriechbaum charged $1.53 a square yard for the brick paving. The curb was made of tooled limestone; Kriechbaum charged 60 cents per linear foot for the curb.

Local newspapers called the road "A Triumph in Practical Engineering." Local legend has it that any horse that galloped up the length of Snake Alley without collapsing was deemed strong enough to pull the town's fire wagons. However, the 21 percent grade of the road meant that horses pulling carriages tired easily and had extra difficulties maneuvering their way up the road. Soon all traffic was routed one-way downhill only. While Snake Alley was considered a unique attraction for Burlington, the design really wasn't that practical, so no more serpentine roads were built.

As of the first part of the twenty-first century, more than one hundred years after the road was built, Snake Alley in Burlington remains an oddity. The original brick remains in place, and, framed by stately Victorian houses on either side, the road harkens back to an Old World style. The Snake Alley Historic District was added to the National Register of Historic Places in 1975 and was named by Ripley's Believe It or Not! as the "Crookedest Street in the World."

PALMER SCHOOL
OF CHIROPRACTIC

1895

Daniel D. Palmer placed the book he had been reading down on his desk and leaned back in his chair. He folded his arms across his wide chest and tipped his bearded face to the ceiling, lost in thought. Palmer's office was on the fourth floor of the Ryan Building at the corner of Second and Brady in downtown Davenport, Iowa. A self-proclaimed researcher of natural healing methods, Palmer had been reading works by the Greek healer Hippocrates. Two quotes caught his eye: "Natural forces within us are the true healers of disease," and "Get knowledge of the spine, for this is the requisite for many diseases."

It was September 1895. Palmer had been living in Davenport for ten years as a natural magnetic healer. Magnetic healing was a non-traditional folk remedy that Palmer offered as an alternative to modern medicine. However, Palmer had recently developed an interest in getting to the root cause of diseases and wanted to develop a way to treat the causes and not just the symptoms.

Palmer was especially intrigued by the idea of spinal manipulation. If trauma to the spine could cause nerves to be pinched, could adjustments of the spinal column restore the normal transmission of nerve impulses? And would that cure medical issues such as asthma and rheumatism?

Palmer stood and grabbed his topcoat. Locking the door to his office behind him, he headed down the stairs to the lobby. When he reached the main level, a loud commotion on the street outside the Ryan Building caught his attention, along with the attention of everyone else in the lobby. But Palmer noticed one man who seemed to be ignoring the ruckus outside. That man was the Ryan Building's janitor, Harvey Lillard. As Palmer soon learned, Lillard was able to ignore the noise from the street because he was deaf.

Lillard had been deaf for seventeen years. He related to Palmer that he suddenly went deaf one day after bending over and hearing a pop in his back. Palmer ran his hands up Lillard's back and thought he felt a slight bump on his spine. Palmer was confident that with a little manipulation, he could adjust the vertebrae and possibly restore Lillard's hearing.

Palmer took Lillard back upstairs to his fourth-floor office. He had Lillard lie down on a table and carefully felt around the bump on Lillard's spine. With a slight thrust, Palmer adjusted the spine. Lillard sat back up with a look of wonder on his face—he could hear again!

Palmer named his new healing strategy *chiropractic*, roughly translated as "done by hand" in Greek. He was encouraged by his son B. J. to train others. Two years later, in 1897, the first official class in chiropractic was held in the newly named Palmer School and Cure. Courses included anatomy, physiology, and practical training. The name was eventually changed to the Palmer School of Chiropractic, and in 1906, B. J. took over as head of the school.

Over the years, more and more students enrolled at the Palmer School of Chiropractic as chiropractors worked to gain acceptance into the medical field. By the 1920s, the school had moved to the 800th block of Brady Street and boasted more than one thousand students. The name was eventually changed again to the Palmer College of Chiropractic.

Mainstream medical practitioners were slow to accept chiropractic as a reliable alternative to drug therapy and care. Many chiropractors were charged with practicing medicine without a license and jailed. In 1913, Kansas became the first state to establish a licensing procedure for chiropractic care; the last state to do so was Louisiana in 1974.

Today, chiropractic is recognized as an official health care profession in all fifty states and many countries. There are more than seventy thousand active chiropractic licenses in the United States alone. The Palmer College of Chiropractic maintains its campus in Davenport and is joined by campuses in Florida and California. The Palmer College of Chiropractic is known as the birthplace of an alternative form of care that is currently utilized by twenty million Americans.

BUXTON
A Town Ahead of Its Time

1900

An editorial in the November 4, 1910, issue of the *Iowa State Bystander*, a Des Moines–based African American newspaper, talked of the progressive and peaceful mining town that was Buxton, Iowa. Buxton, located in Bluff Creek Township, Monroe County, was a unique community. From 1900 to the early 1920s, Buxton, Iowa, was a predominantly black yet fully integrated community, the only one of its kind in Iowa and perhaps throughout the Midwest.

The editorial put it best by saying, "Go and see the Negro and his white companion, working in peace and harmony, hand in hand, in their daily labor unions, in schools, and stores, in shops, and in the mines."

Buxton was a coal mining town established in 1900 by the Consolidation Coal Company, a subsidiary of the Chicago & North Western Railroad. Instead of the normal camp-like setup common with mining towns, Buxton was actually strategically planned and methodically platted, complete with water and utilities, an artificial lake, schools, churches, and even a three-story YMCA equipped with heat and electricity.

What really made Buxton unique was that in addition to the mostly black miners, the town was filled with black merchants, business owners, accountants, teachers, doctors, lawyers, pharmacists, and cigar makers. There were also Swedish, Slovakian, and Welsh immigrants. Integration of the town started in the mines and continued into the neighborhoods, schools, and social venues.

Beginning in 1880, the Consolidation Coal Company recruited mostly black miners from Virginia and West Virginia to come to Iowa, originally creating the settlement of Muchakinock, south of Oskaloosa. By the late 1900s, the mines around Muchakinock were depleted and a new settlement in Buxton was planned. As housing became available in Buxton, the miners transferred there from Muchakinock. Soon Muchakinock was abandoned and Buxton thrived.

Buxton residents could either rent company-built houses at $7 or $8 a month or they could purchase acreage from the company and build their own homes. Most lots had space for large gardens and even room to raise chickens and pigs.

The miners rode to and from the mines daily on a local railroad built for that purpose. A prominent building in town was the Company Store, which employed up to eighty people, both black and white. Buxton residents shopped for ladies' wear, drugs, shoes, hardware, mining tools, and groceries at the Company Store. The groceries were standard general store items: sugar and flour in large sacks and butter, lard, vinegar, kraut, and peanut butter in large containers. The exact amounts needed were measured out for each customer.

Buxton was named after the Consolidation Coal Company superintendent at the time, Ben C. Buxton. The twenty-five-year-old Buxton personally took on the responsibility of laying out the town. By 1908, less than ten years after its founding, Buxton boasted five thousand residents, reaching a peak population of eight to ten thousand residents in the 1910s.

One famous resident of Buxton was E. A. Carter. The son of a black miner, Carter became the first black graduate of the University of Iowa Medical College in 1907. He returned home to Buxton as the assistant chief surgeon for Consolidation Coal Company and, by 1915, had moved up to chief surgeon.

Buxton also had its own baseball team, the Buxton Wonders. The Wonders started out as an all-black team but soon integrated whites to play with them. Their largest field in town was called the Amphitheater. The Wonders were reported to be an excellent team, beating the much-favored Chicago Union Giants 6-1 in a 1909 matchup.

The sudden appearance of Buxton on the Iowa prairie in 1900 was dwarfed only by its sudden disappearance. In the early 1920s, the town was abandoned after the Consolidation Coal Company moved its base of operations. By 1927, the town was empty.

An archaeological dig in 1980 found the remains of the once-thriving community in the form of china, personal care items, cooking utensils, toys, and household goods. Archaeologists also located the town's cemetery and unearthed the remains of houses and buildings. In fifty short years, this parcel of land in northern Monroe County went from empty prairie to the largest coal mining community in Iowa and back to empty prairie.

A BUTTER COW IS BORN

1911

John Daniels leaned back on his three-legged stool and admired his work. After hours of smearing, shaping, and crafting, he was finished. Towering above him as he sat crouched on the stool was his latest masterpiece.

"You are a beauty," Daniels murmured, smoothing down one last ridge.

Daniels stood and stretched, shivering in the cold glass case. The room was kept at 35 degrees Fahrenheit so his medium wouldn't melt. Daniels slowly circled his carving, marveling at the curve of the ribs, the slight flaring of the nostrils. The Norwegian immigrant had been doing sculptures like this for more than a decade, but he thought this one might be his favorite. Using only butter on top of a metal and wood frame, Daniels had created a life-size, six hundred-pound replica of a cow. Next to the cow was a butter-carved replica of a small boy and a calf. Daniels had positioned the boy so that he appeared to be leading the calf to its mother's milk.

Cow, calf, and boy were ready to be displayed at the Iowa State Fair.

The year was 1911. John K. Daniels had been tasked by the organizers of the Iowa State Fair to create a sculpture out of butter that would be the envy of the surrounding states. Butter sculpting had been gaining popularity in recent years, and the Iowa State Fair organizers wanted something to wow the crowds. The Beatrice Creamery Co. of Des Moines sponsored the nationally known Daniels to do the work.

The Iowa State Fair had been going strong annually since 1854. It had moved from Fairfield and other towns in the eastern part of the state to Des Moines by the late 1870s. Every year it grew a little bigger and attracted more and more people. Fair organizers were sure that the butter sculpture would promote Iowa's dairy farm heritage and draw in extra crowds.

It worked. The first butter cow drew in hundreds of visitors. Daniels was followed by Nebraska sculptor and taxidermist J. E. Wallace, who was also well known on the butter sculpting circuit. Wallace spent most of his adult life traveling the Midwest with his sculptures, including working at county and state fairs in Texas, Kansas, Nebraska, Ohio, Illinois, Kentucky, and Tennessee.

Wallace sculpted a new butter cow, plus additional figures, every year until his death in 1956. In 1957, Earl Frank Dutt of Illinois took over the responsibility of creating the attraction. Dutt was a trained sculptor who had attended the Art Institute of Chicago.

In 1958, a Toledo, Iowa, dairy farm wife named Norma Lyon, commonly known as Duffy, saw a picture of Dutt's work and scoffed. She felt she could do a better job and told the Iowa State Fair director that exact thing. The director encouraged her to apprentice under Dutt in 1959, which she did. In 1960, Duffy Lyon became the premier Butter Cow Lady on her own.

Duffy Lyon took her work seriously, but also took a few creative liberties with her butter allotment. Every year saw a new cow, always a dairy breed, but the cows were joined by likenesses of famous people, like Garth Brooks and Elvis, or popular scenes, like the Peanuts gang or a full-size depiction of Leonardo da Vinci's *The Last Supper*.

Duffy retired in 2005 and was replaced in 2006 by her apprentice of fifteen years, Sarah Pratt of West Des Moines.

With each new artist, the Iowa State Fair Butter Cow and accompanying display varies. However, each sculptor uses the same basic process. They start with a wood and metal framework in the shape of a cow, approximately five and a half feet high and eight feet long. Six hundred pounds of unsalted cream butter are brought to 40 degrees Fahrenheit. Sculpting starts with the head and neck, with the artist adding layer after layer of butter. The artist then moves to the body and down the legs to the hooves. The goal is to make the cow look as realistic as possible—artists even depict the veins in the cow's udder.

With refrigeration, the sculpture can last more than six months. A new butter cow is created every year, often using the melted-down butter from the previous year. Approximately one million people pass by the butter cow's refrigerated display case at the Iowa State Fair each year.

The Iowa State Fair remains the single largest event in the state. It has inspired a novel, three movies, and a Broadway musical. The state fairgrounds is even on the National Register of Historic Places. But most visitors to the fair don't care about all that. They just want to see a life-size cow made of butter.

LADY LIBERTY AT CAMP DODGE

1918

Camp Dodge was already stirring by the time the sun rose on Thursday, August 22, 1918. The men had completed drill and eaten breakfast. Most of the conversation around the camp centered on the big event scheduled for that afternoon.

Camp Dodge was the site of the 13th National Army Cantonment, a place where soldiers from throughout the United States were stationed to train prior to service abroad in the Great War. Up until June 15, 1917, the camp had been the home of the Iowa National Guard. When the United States officially entered the Great War, Des Moines had petitioned to be one of the cities chosen to host training camps for US soldiers. The petition was granted and Camp Dodge was selected.

Seemingly overnight, a full-service US Army base appeared. Before the end of the summer of 1917, Camp Dodge boasted fifteen hundred buildings, including barracks, warehouses, a power plant, a YMCA, a Jewish Welfare Society organization, and a five-hundred-bed hospital. The army developed all the plans and hired a local workforce to complete it.

The first soldiers arrived on September 5, 1917, and for the next year and a half, until the end of the war in late 1918, Camp Dodge witnessed 150,000 soldiers on her training grounds, a third of whom were Iowa citizens. Those soldiers, in addition to learning the art of war, took advantage of other camp offerings such as clubs, sports, and concerts.

In August 1918, Camp Dodge was visited by two gentlemen from Chicago. Their names were Arthur Mole and John Thomas. Mole and Thomas had made a name for themselves in the past year as photographers, showing up at army bases and naval training centers around the country. Mole and Thomas used the soldiers and officers at those locations to create what they called "living photographs." The men, and sometimes women, were arranged in methodical and precise positions that, when viewed from a significant distance, coalesced into a dramatic, patriotic symbol.

Since the US entry into the Great War in 1917, Mole and Thomas had created more than thirty such patriotic images. A visit to Camp Lee in Virginia netted them a living Uncle Sam. More than thirty thousand officers and men created a US Shield at Camp Custer in Battle Creek, Michigan. Enlisted men at the Marine Barracks at Parris Island, South Carolina, formed their own Marine emblem. At Camp Dix, New Jersey, twenty-five thousand officers and men formed the human Liberty Bell, complete with a crack. Now it was Camp Dodge's turn.

The setup at Camp Dodge took several days. First, a forty-foot tower was erected at one end of a parade ground. Using thousands of yards of white tape, the outline of the image slowly took shape. It was the Statue of Liberty.

Starting at 1:00 p.m. on August 22, soldiers began appearing on the parade ground. The temperatures hovered just under 100 degrees Fahrenheit, and most of the men were in full uniform. By the time all eighteen thousand men were situated inside the outline, it was after 2:00 p.m. A dozen soldiers fainted in the heat and had to be carted off the field.

From the top of that forty-foot tower, instructions were shouted down to the field. To make the shades apparent in the Statue of Liberty's gown, random groups of soldiers were asked to remove their jackets and expose their white shirts. More soldiers were moved up to Lady Liberty's torch; the increased density of men in that space helped solidify the perspective.

At 2:30 p.m., Mole and Thomas were ready to take the picture. They stood atop the tower and gazed down at Lady Liberty. It was the longest image they had attempted—the distance from her feet to the top of the torch was nearly half a mile.

The photograph was a success. Postcards were made of the image, which soldiers purchased for a dollar. Many were sent home as mementos. Still others were used for propaganda.

Just three months after the Statue of Liberty photograph was taken, on November 11, 1918, the armistice to end fighting in the Great War was signed. One month after that, Camp Dodge became a demobilization facility.

In the months following the end of the war, nearly 210,000 soldiers again passed through Camp Dodge, this time on their way back home. Soon Camp Dodge was deserted. Some buildings were auctioned off and some were dismantled. Camp Dodge is still in use today as the headquarters of the Iowa National Guard.

I SCREAM, YOU SCREAM,
WE ALL SCREAM FOR ICE CREAM

1920

Christian Nelson smiled as he handed the ice cream cone to the little girl on the other side of the counter.

"One vanilla ice cream cone," Christian announced. "That will be five cents."

The little girl's father reached into his suit pocket and took out a nickel. Placing it into Christian's outstretched hand, he said thank you, then led his daughter to a small table by the front of the shop.

Christian absentmindedly wiped down the counter with a towel as he gazed out the big picture window at the front of his store. He could see quite a bit of downtown Onawa from where he was, and he enjoyed watching the residents of the small community stroll up and down the wide main street while he manned the counter of his confectionery shop. During his day job teaching at the local high school, the twenty-seven-year old was focused on educating young minds, but once he donned the apron at his store after school, he was able to interact with the rest of the population of Onawa, which in 1920 numbered just over twenty-two hundred.

Christian Nelson's family emigrated from Denmark to the United States in 1893 when Christian was just an infant. They settled in Iowa and became dairy farmers. Christian knew that wasn't the life for him, so he had gone to the University of Nebraska and earned a teaching certificate, finishing school in 1916. He served in World War I until the war's end in 1918, and then accepted a teaching position in Onawa. To supplement his income, he had opened a small ice cream shop.

Things were going well for Christian, but recently he had felt restless, unsure if teaching was the right profession for him. Sighing, Christian grabbed a broom and started sweeping behind the counter.

The front door of the shop opened. Christian looked up to see a young boy walk in slowly, his left hand clenched into a fist. Christian smiled at the boy and beckoned him to approach the counter.

"What can I get for you?" he asked.

The boy turned his head and caught sight of the girl and her father. The girl was still enjoying her ice cream cone, giggling as a drop landed on her wrist. The boy looked back up at Christian and said, "I think I want an ice cream cone."

Christian grabbed the metal scoop and said, "One ice cream cone . . . coming right up!"

"Wait!" the boy said suddenly. Christian paused with the scoop hovering just above the creamy batch of ice cream. The boy was looking at the different kinds of chocolate piled up in the glass display case in front of him.

"Um . . . I guess I would rather have a chocolate bar," the boy said.

"Are you sure?" Christian asked.

"Well, I really want both," the boy said. Then he held out his left fist and spread his fingers to show a single dull nickel in his palm.

"But I only have five cents to spend," he said, "and together they would cost ten cents, right?"

Christian smiled at the boy. "You are correct."

The boy nodded and stared at the display case a little while longer. Finally he looked up at Christian and said, "Yup, I just want the chocolate bar. Maybe I'll get the ice cream next time."

Several hours later, Christian locked the door behind his last customer and started cleaning up the shop. He wiped down the tables and chairs and swept the floor. He covered the trays of treats in the display case and hung his apron on a hook by the register. As he gathered up his coat and hat and walked toward the rear exit of the store, Christian thought again about the boy from earlier in the day. As he flipped the lock on the back of the store, Christian paused.

"What if I combined them?" he wondered aloud. "What if I made a chocolate bar with ice cream on the inside?"

Christian pondered this on his slow walk home. He thought about it as he washed his face and trimmed his mustache. He dwelled on it as he slipped into bed.

The next few weeks were a blur of experiments for Christian as he tried, unsuccessfully, to create a chocolate-covered ice cream bar. He still taught at the high school and ran his confectionery store, but a corner of his mind was constantly generating ideas on how to fix his main problem: getting the melted chocolate to stick to the frozen ice cream.

Finally, Christian did it. He found a perfect measurement of cocoa butter that would work as an edible adhesive between the chocolate and the ice cream. Christian was pleased with the results, but knew he needed to test them.

Christian volunteered to provide a special treat for the upcoming Onawa Fireman's Tournament. He worked after hours to create five hundred of what he called I-Scream Bars.

The day of the Fireman's Tournament dawned bright and sunny. Christian nervously paced back and forth under the white tent he had erected to sell his bars. Soon the crowds started coming, and business was brisk. At the end of the picnic, Christian opened his basket to count how many I-Scream Bars he had left and was astounded to discover they were all gone. He had sold out.

Taking a leap of faith, Christian quit his teaching job in Onawa, closed up his confectionery shop, and, with recipe in hand, moved to nearby Omaha, Nebraska, to find a manufacturing partner. On July 13, 1921, Christian met with a chocolate maker and pitched his I-Scream Bars. The chocolate maker, a man by the name of Russell Stover, was so impressed that he drafted a partnership contract that same day. Stover, who was managing the Graham Ice Cream Company office in Omaha, convinced Christian to add a stick as a handle on the frozen treat and rename it Eskimo Pie.

The two immediately got to work, deciding to test the Eskimo Pie in both Des Moines and Omaha by summer's end. The treat hit the collective sweet spot of midwesterners; at one point that summer, a quarter of a million Eskimo Pies were sold in Omaha during a twenty-four-hour period.

The two men moved to Chicago and began to nationally market the Eskimo Pie. By the beginning of 1922, Christian reported that Eskimo Pies were sold in each of the forty-eight states, and daily production had reached four million.

Patent issues dogged the Eskimo Pie. Christian had been granted a patent in January 1922, but soon was spending $4,000 a day to defend it. Stover sold his shares back to Christian, who then turned to R. S. Reynolds for help. Reynolds owned the U.S. Foil Company and had been providing the foil wrappers for the Eskimo Pies. In 1924, Reynolds's company became the sole owner of the Eskimo Pie.

Christian retired a very wealthy young man, but found he missed his work. In 1935, he rejoined the company and worked on innovations, including special holiday-themed shapes and colors of the Eskimo Pie. In 1955, he was awarded another patent for his Eskimo Machine. The contraption automatically formed the ice cream into standard-size bars and streamlined the manufacturing process.

Christian Nelson never went back to teaching, but his defining life's work was sparked by a desire to make one child happy.

TAKING TO THE SKIES

1920

Neta Snook stood back from her plane, looking it over. Finally. After years of tinkering, years of studying, years of instruction, today was the day she was going to fly solo.

The twenty-four-year-old aviatrix glanced around. There was her father, whose face reflected an internal mix of pride and apprehension. Next to him stood her mother, nervously chewing on her lower lip as she held the shoulders of Neta's young sister, Vivian. Vivian, for her part, was simply gaping in awe at the plane in front of her.

Neta slipped her helmet over her red curls and adjusted the strap beneath her chin. Next came the goggles. Finally, she cinched the belt tighter on her leather flight jacket. The time had come.

Stepping lightly on the wing of her restored Canuck, Neta hesitated only briefly before settling in the second seat. This was where the instructor normally sat. For the last four years, ever since she started at the flying school in Davenport in 1916, Neta had sat up front. Neta tested the switches and levers in front of her, making sure all parts of the biplane moved as they were supposed to.

Neta and her plane sat at the end of a long pasture just outside Iowa State College in Ames. The Snook family lived on Wilson Avenue, close to downtown. Neta had had to take apart the plane to transport it from her backyard, where it had been for the past two years, to this field for its first run. Now that it was put back together and in apparent working order, Neta could take off on her first solo flight.

Neta's thoughts were not on her own safety, but on the structural worthiness of her craft. Neta had logged hundreds of hours in the air during the last four years, and she had no doubt that she could fly this plane. It was, however, the first plane she had rebuilt on her own, even though she felt as if she had been preparing for this moment her whole life.

Anita Snook was born February 14, 1896, in Illinois. As a young girl, Neta—as she was called—showed a high aptitude for all things mechanical, something that her father encouraged. In 1905, when Neta was nine, the Snook family became owners of a single-seater Stanley Steamer automobile, which owed its name to the fact that it was powered by a steam engine. Father and daughter spent hours poring over the instruction manual, learning the ins and outs of the vehicle. Next they purchased a Kissel Kar, complete with gas-powered lights. The family moved to Ames, Iowa, in 1915, and Neta started classes at Iowa State College. Her dad had secured an Overland Touring car for her to use at school. The Iowa State College administration hesitated to give Neta permission to have the car on campus, expressing concern about the independence it would give the freshman. They finally agreed that Neta could use the vehicle at school, and limited her to female passengers only.

Like all women at Iowa State College in 1915, Neta studied Home Economics. She also, however, increased her class load to twenty-three credit hours each semester by adding on electives such as Mechanical Drawing, Internal Combustion Engines, and Repair and Maintenance of Farm Tractors.

In 1916, during Neta's second year at Iowa State, she heard about a new flying school called the Atlantic Coast Aeronautical Station in Newport News, Virginia. The school had opened the year before under the direction of aviation pioneer Glenn Curtiss. Neta applied, but was immediately rejected. The terse note back from the school simply read, "No Females Allowed."

Not to be discouraged, Neta applied at the Davenport School of Aviation. She was accepted, and after having secured the $400 tuition fee from her mom (against the wishes of her father), Neta left Iowa State and headed to Davenport, Iowa. It was June 1917.

It was at the Davenport School of Aviation that Neta first took to the sky. Even though she was the only girl in a class of about thirty students, Neta—who was nicknamed "Curly" by her classmates—fit right in. The class was working on building a biplane to use for flying lessons. Neta had her first flight on that biplane, with an instructor sitting right behind her, on July 21, 1917.

More flight time followed, but so did disaster. In September of that year, a fatal accident with the biplane closed the school. Encouraged by her classmates, Neta reapplied at the Atlantic Coast Aeronautical Station in Newport News and, this time, was accepted. To save money, Neta sneaked onto a freight train late one night and headed to Virginia.

Neta's time in Newport News was short-lived. America decided to enter the Great War raging in Europe, and all non-military flying was banned. Neta eventually moved back home to Ames in 1918. The war ended in November 1918, but by that time, Neta had purchased a wrecked Canadian training plane and was in the process of restoring it in her parent's backyard.

Now it was spring of 1920 and the Canuck was ready to go. Neta sat in the open cockpit and gave a thumbs-up to her friend standing in front of the plane. The friend nodded back, reached up to grasp the propeller, and, with a loud grunt, swung it around. It caught, and Neta smiled at the vibrating purr of the engine. Soon she was in the air on her first solo flight.

Throughout that spring and summer, Neta barnstormed all across Iowa and into the surrounding states, giving fifteen-minute rides to passengers for $15. Many of the people Neta met that summer had never seen a plane before, much less one piloted by a woman.

As the summer wound down, Neta was awarded an official pilot's license, making her Iowa's first female aviator. When she noticed that her license listed her passenger carry count as NONE, Neta carefully erased the first letter, turning the word into ONE.

Neta earned enough money that, as the weather turned colder, she was able to pay for her plane to be dismantled and shipped by boxcar to Los Angeles. Neta hoped the warm California climate would allow her to continue flying year-round.

Once she reached California, Neta found a job at Kinner Airport, which was owned by another Iowa transplant, Bert Kinner. She was soon working as a flight instructor and commercial pilot. In late December 1920, Neta met the person who was to become her most famous pupil.

Years later, in her autobiography, Neta recalled her first meeting with the tall, slender young lady. Neta remembers the woman said she had sought out Neta to appease her parents, thinking a female instructor would make them feel better about their daughter's insistence on learning to fly. On January 3, 1921, Neta took the young lady up in the air for her first lesson. By the time they landed, the pupil, Amelia Earhart, was hooked.

For the rest of 1921 and the first part of 1922, Neta and Amelia were never far apart. They flew together often, first in Neta's plane, than in Amelia's. The two became fast friends, and when Neta was one of forty pilots to enter a men's air race at the Los Angeles Speedway in February 1921, Amelia was there to cheer Neta to a fifth-place finish.

Amelia was just about to solo for the first time in mid-1922 when Neta announced her retirement from flying. Neta, recently married to Bill Southern, had just found out she was pregnant and decided to ground herself permanently. Neta Snook Southern's last time in the cockpit was in August 1922.

Neta dropped out of the spotlight as Amelia grew more and more popular. In 1937, the news broke that Amelia Earhart and her plane had disappeared somewhere over the Pacific Ocean on Amelia's attempt to fly around the world. Neta was devastated.

In 1974, Neta published her autobiography, titled *I Taught Amelia to Fly*. She began touring the country, giving lectures and presentations about her history in aviation. After nearly two decades of touring, Neta Snook Southern passed away in 1991 at the age of ninety-five.

In 1992, Neta was inducted into the Iowa Aviation Hall of Fame in Greenfield, Iowa. She is remembered as an aviation adventurer and as the pilot who taught Amelia Earhart how to fly.

THE MUSIC MAN OF FORT DODGE

1920

The tall young man at the podium raised his hands. Immediately, the band members fell silent and brought their instruments to the ready. All eyes were on the conductor as he ticked off the march tempo with his baton.

At his downbeat, the band came alive. They were playing one of the conductor's compositions, and this was as much an audition for them as it was for the conductor. If the band liked this conductor and the conductor liked this band, a contract would be drawn up and the Iowa Military Band of Fort Dodge would have a new leader in Karl King.

Fort Dodge had had a band for a generation. One early director was Carl Quist, a Danish immigrant who had come to Fort Dodge around 1900. He took the band, then known as the 56th Regiment Band affiliated with the Iowa National Guard, on the road, adding contests, fairs, and exhibitions throughout the Midwest and even into Canada to their schedule. When they were home in Fort

Dodge, the band played year-round, performing a majority of their concerts on street corners.

In 1911, the band split from the Iowa National Guard and became known as the Iowa Military Band. By 1920, the band was looking for a new director and set up an audition concert for Karl King. King had arrived a few days prior to the concert at the City Park Square in Fort Dodge and had run several rehearsals as a guest director. Now it was showtime.

Karl King was no stranger to directing in front of strangers. Born in 1891 in Paintersville, Ohio, King developed an early interest in music, taking cornet and baritone lessons. He quit school after the eighth grade, published his first march at age sixteen, and, at age nineteen, joined a circus band, spending the next several years traveling the country. Although King had taken music lessons as a child, he had no formal training in either composition or conducting. During one circus performance, the band director became ill and King was selected to take his place. He never went back to playing in the band, noting to friends that "waving that little stick is a hell of a lot easier than blowing that damn big baritone horn."

King rubbed elbows with some of the most famous entertainers of his day. He played for Buffalo Bill Cody and his Wild West Show. He wrote a circus march that was given the title "Barnum & Bailey's Favorite." In 1917, King was asked by John Ringling of the Ringling Bros. Circus to form a new band for their company, as they had lost most of their original band members to the war effort.

Luckily for the citizens of Fort Dodge, by 1920 King was ready to get out of the circus life, mostly because of the disapproval of his in-laws. The audition concert in Fort Dodge during the summer of 1920 was a success. King was offered a one-year contract, worth $2,500, to direct the Iowa Military Band of Fort Dodge. He accepted.

King arrived in Fort Dodge on October 1, 1920, to start his new position. The band was small, with only eighteen members. Four days after his arrival, on October 5, the band was scheduled to appear in a parade in Fort Dodge. After that, they would have a few months to prepare for their next concert in January 1921.

That fall, King invited former circus friends to join him in Fort Dodge, extolling the virtues of small-town living. By the time the January 21, 1921, concert at the Princess Theatre rolled around, the band was back up to thirty-five members.

Karl King soon found himself fitting right in to life in Fort Dodge. He continued to compose, eventually claiming over three hundred pieces to his name. King focused mainly on marches, but his circus background gave his marches more of a lively feel than traditional military marches. When listening to a King march, one can almost see horses galloping around the ring, picture trapeze artists swinging back and forth, and imagine acrobats running and tumbling.

In 1923, King's wife, Ruth, opened the Ruth King Music Shoppe in Fort Dodge, which served as both a music store and a publishing shop. King traveled quite a bit with the band, but was always happy to return home to Fort Dodge, to his family, and to the Karl King Koffee Klatch, which was a group of men who met daily at a local cafe for coffee and conversation.

During 1921, his first full year in Fort Dodge, King did more than just direct the band. He, along with fellow band leaders Alonzo Leach and Major George Landers, lobbied the Iowa Legislature to pass the Iowa Band Law. The bill would allow cities to increase local property taxes to support a local band. Thanks to King and the others, the bill passed in late 1921. The next November, Fort Dodge voters passed the Band Tax in their community; during the rest of the 1920s, it generated approximately $8,000 a year for the Iowa Military Band.

Perhaps because of his work with the Iowa Band Law, King and the band itself both neglected to do something quite important in October 1921. That was when King's one-year contract was up. Neither King nor the band moved to renew the contract; nevertheless, King stayed as the leader of the band for the next fifty years.

The 1920s and 1930s were golden years for municipal bands. The military-style uniforms worn by King and the band members invoked a sense of patriotic pride in the audience, as did King's habit of ending every concert with "The Star-Spangled Banner." The band played at fairs and marched in parades throughout Iowa and the Midwest.

In 1929, King was president of the Iowa Band Masters' Association. He scheduled the organization's annual meetings for early May 1930. King decided to start a concert to go with the meetings and called it Northwest Iowa's Band Jubilee. On May 8, 1930, twelve municipal bands marched in a long parade down Central Avenue in Fort Dodge. More than 350 musicians were involved. Some say there were 76 trombones that led the parade, with 110 cornets right behind. Whether or not the Northwest Iowa's Band Jubilee was the inspiration for *The Music Man* is still debated, but Fort Dodge citizens who attended that first jubilee were moved and astounded by the spectacle.

As the Fort Dodge Municipal Band, as it had become known, entered its third decade under the direction of Karl King in the 1940s, things were beginning to change. The advent of World War II cut into the band's numbers, and state and county fairs were cancelled for the duration of the war. King started accepting women into the band to fill it and, after the city of Fort Dodge built them a band shell in Oleson Park, the Fort Dodge Municipal Band started staying home more instead of going on tour.

Karl King was named as Iowa's outstanding citizen in 1951, but the glory days of municipal bands were fading. By the 1960s, audiences had dwindled due to a shift in musical tastes and an increase in other entertainment options. King suffered a mild heart attack in 1965 and, even though he was still directing in 1970, was forced to take sips of oxygen before and after concerts.

On March 31, 1971, after more than fifty years in front of the Fort Dodge Municipal Band, Karl King passed away. The band played on and soon formally adopted a new name. They are now known as the Karl L. King Municipal Band. On certain summer nights, King's legacy can still be heard drifting on the Fort Dodge air as a new generation of musicians continues to perform his lively marches.

IOWA HIGH SCHOOL
GIRLS BASKETBALL

1920

As the clock wound down, the Correctionville Girls High School basketball team was getting ready to celebrate. It was March 12, 1920, and the Correctionville team was just about to become the very first state champions in Iowa in girls high school basketball. They were finishing up their fifth game in two days and, after playing so many games and spending the night sleeping on the floor on wrestling mats in the Drake University Fieldhouse, were ready to return to their town of one thousand people with the title.

Correctionville, a small town near Sioux City, Iowa, had not lost a single girls basketball game in two years. They were now up on a team from Nevada, Iowa, with a score of 11-4 with less than ten seconds on the clock. Of the twenty-four teams competing in the first state tournament—all of which were from small, rural communities—Correctionville was undoubtedly the best.

Even though tournament officials had shortened the game from its regular two twenty-minute halves to two ten-minute halves to not overwork the girls, the team was exhausted. Their uniforms, which included pleated bloomers with elastic at the knees, heavy wool stockings, and a buttoned-up blouse with full sleeves, cuffs, and a sailor collar, were drenched with sweat.

Correctionville coach Daisy Marsten watched the clock tick down to zero. She knew she and her team were making history. There was already talk of discontinuing girls athletics at the high school level across the nation due to fears that exercise was not good for the female body. Marsten knew how popular basketball was in Iowa's many small towns, though, so she wasn't worried.

Finally, it was over. The team from Correctionville had won the Iowa state championship. The girls boarded the night train to return to Correctionville with a portion of the profits made at the tournament: a whopping $2.43. More importantly, an annual event showcasing the best in Iowa girls high school basketball had been established, which continues to this day.

Basketball began in 1891 when James Naismith of Springfield, Massachusetts, wanted to create a fun, indoor game college boys could play. The sport was popular from the beginning with both males and females; by 1893, the Dubuque YMCA had started a girls' league.

Rules of the game were not standardized until the turn of the twentieth century and often varied from town to town. When a set of rules was finally agreed upon, Iowa girls teams ended up with six players from each team on the court.

The court was divided into three segments, with the goals at either end separated by a center section. The ball could only be dribbled twice before being passed to another player or put up for a shot. The players could not cross center court, so some players only played offense (forwards) and some only played defense (guards). The guard couldn't strip the ball away from shooters outside the lane. Also, the girls were forbidden from having any bodily contact with each other. Fouls were few and considered very poor sportsmanship.

The ball itself was easily deflated, and the stitches had a tendency to come loose after a while. The baskets at each end of the court were actual baskets; spectators in the balconies behind the baskets had to reach down and retrieve the ball if a shot was made. After each basket, the ball was carried to the center of the court for a jump shot to restart play. Oftentimes, the girls teams played outside, as the indoor courts were reserved for the boys. If that was the case, a long pole was brought out to pop the ball out of the basket if a shot was made.

In 1925, five years after the inaugural girls basketball tournament, the Iowa High School Athletic Association (IHSAA) announced at their annual meeting that they were going to cease sponsorship of all girls basketball programs and that the playing of competitive sports before a paying crowd would be limited to boys athletics. The move by the IHSAA was partially in response to a growing national trend of curtailing girls' athletics.

Just a few weeks after the IHSAA's announcement, twenty-five small-school administrators from throughout Iowa joined together and formed the new Iowa Girls High School Athletic Union (IGHSAU). This organization was formed with the sole purpose of overseeing high school basketball for girls in the state.

In 1926, during their first year in existence, the IGHSAU had a membership of 159 high schools from all over the state. Nearly all were small, rural schools.

Despite the popular belief that girls should not engage in such strenuous activity, girls high school basketball in Iowa flourished. By 1932, the heavy, full bloomers were no longer worn; instead, the girls switched to satin shorts. The change took place to accommodate not only evolving fashions, but also the Great Depression—limited money for most families meant they couldn't buy extra fabric for the bloomers.

In 1934, the three-section court disappeared and the current two-section court came into use. Still, Iowa teams featured six players on each side with three on offense and three on defense, each delegated to their own half of the court.

By the 1940s, 70 percent of Iowa high school girls played basketball. In addition, 70 percent of those teams had a school population of fewer than one hundred students. The 1949 state tournament had more than forty thousand spectators, and the 1951 tournament was the first Iowa high school event to be televised statewide. *Sports Illustrated* called Iowa a utopia for girls' athletics.

However, the winds of change were blowing. In 1969, the University of Iowa held a special basketball clinic to introduce Iowa girls high school coaches to the five-player format that boys and collegiate players used. Three years later, with the passing of the Education Act of 1972, or Title IX, schools were required to offer the same activity opportunities for both boys and girls. That led the large schools, which had previously stayed out of the IGHSAU, to start up their basketball programs. Beginning in 1984, schools could choose to play either with the five-player rules as we know them today, or with the traditional six-player rules Iowans had been using for more than fifty years. Most large schools chose the five-player option, while the small, rural schools stayed with what they knew.

All that changed, however, in February 1993 when the IGHSAU voted to completely discontinue six-player basketball in the state of Iowa. Thousands of high schools girls had to learn the game from scratch the next season.

Iowa girls played six-player basketball for one hundred years, from 1893 to 1993. They were the second-to-last state in the United States to offer six-player basketball; Oklahoma dropped their program two years later. The IGHSAU continued to serve Iowa girls, adding softball to their organization in 1955, golf and tennis in 1956, track and field in 1962, swimming and diving in 1967, and volleyball in 1970. Recent additions include soccer in 1998 and bowling in 2006.

When the IGHSAU was created in 1926, it was the first and only organization in America solely dedicated to supporting girls high school sports. The IGHSAU is still in operation today and is the longest-lasting high school athletic association for females.

ENTERTAINING
WITH TRAIN WRECKS

1932

"Welcome to the Fair of Thrills!"

"Git yer candy here!"

"Over here, over here! Ride the midway!"

Attendees at the 1932 Iowa State Fair in Des Moines were overwhelmed with the sights, sounds, and smells surrounding them. Young boys darted between crowds of people, trying to maneuver close to whatever was drawing the most attention. This year, it promised to be the staged train collision in the grandstand.

The man in charge of the collision was Iowa native Joseph Connolly. Connolly was bringing his thrilling event to the Iowa State Fair for the third time. He had staged the first one in 1896, followed by one in 1922. Now, ten years later, Iowans were flocking to the grandstand to witness the latest collision. Some remembered the spectacle from before; others had heard the stories.

Connolly was going to make sure that the 1932 collision would be one to remember. In honor of the upcoming presidential election, he had painted the name *Hoover* on one of the steam locomotives that would be used in the crash, and *Roosevelt* on the other. The locomotives each weighed about one hundred tons, but Connolly had taken extra steps to make sure the event would be memorable. He had inclined the track at each end to help the locomotives pick up speed, and loaded them with dynamite and open barrels of gasoline.

Hoover and *Roosevelt* were going to be blown sky high.

Connolly had gotten bit by the destruction bug in 1896 when he saw a staged head-on train collision in Missouri. William Crush, the aptly named vice president of the Missouri, Kansas, and Texas Railroad, dreamed up the collision as a way to make scrap metal out of two old locomotives. He billed it as a unique entertainment opportunity, and the crowds flocked to see it happen.

The crash in Missouri did not go as Crush had planned. The explosion was larger than he anticipated and the damage more widespread. After the smoke cleared, two spectators lay dead and many more were injured.

The fatalities didn't dissuade Connolly from approaching the Iowa State Fair organizers with a proposal to do something similar at the fair that year. He vowed to take complete responsibility for the event, insisting that there was a better way to stage the crashes to minimize or even eliminate injuries. One of Connolly's best suggestions included erecting barriers in front of the crash site to keep the crowds back.

The Iowa State Fair board accepted his proposal, and it went off without a hitch.

After that first collision in 1896, Connolly started traveling the nation staging crashes. He estimated that between 1896 and 1932, he masterminded seventy-three train collisions at state fairs and exhibitions—causing the destruction of 146 locomotives. The crowds loved it; Connolly once remarked that "somewhere in the makeup of every normal person there lurks the suppressed desire to smash things up."

The collision at the Iowa State Fair in 1932 drew between forty and seventy thousand spectators, depending on who you ask. The entire fair that year had been built on the idea of excitement; the theme was even "A Fair of Thrills." Fair organizers were attempting to lure people to come to the fair at a time when many, still in the throes of the Great Depression, simply did not (or could not) place a high priority on entertainment.

Connolly started the act with a demolition derby he called Safety Demonstrations. Once the crowd had witnessed several automobile crashes, the two locomotives were set in place. *Roosevelt* came in from the left, while *Hoover* picked up speed from the right. Because of the inclined track, the locomotives were traveling at an estimated fifty miles per hour when they collided.

The initial sound of the collision was overshadowed by the bright explosion that happened a heartbeat later. Clouds of smoke rolled off the locomotives and over the fairgrounds. There was massive destruction, but to Connolly's confusion, very few cheers.

Connolly thought he was giving the crowds what they wanted, but he was wrong. Interest in watching a staged train collision was waning, and with so many Iowans still affected by the Great Depression, the entire show seemed like a giant waste. Later, word leaked out that Connolly had charged the Iowa State Fair $40,000 to put on his event. The public was disgusted at such a large expenditure for something so destructive. It also didn't help when the public learned that the Iowa State Fair lost more than $65,000 overall on the fair that year.

After the 1932 Iowa State Fair fiasco, Connolly retired from the train collision business. The Iowa State Fair still hosts events at the grandstand, and some involve crashes, but none are as destructive as a head-on train collision.

DUTCH REAGAN ON THE RADIO

1932

"And that's your ballgame, folks. The final score for the 1932 Home-coming game is the Minnesota Golden Gophers 21, your Iowa Hawkeyes 6. Broadcasting live from Iowa Stadium in Iowa City for WOC Radio in Davenport, I'm Dutch Reagan."

Dutch pulled the headphone away from his ear and gently placed the microphone on the table in front of him. He looked out of the press box and across the field. The Iowa Hawkeyes, shoulders slumped in defeat, were huddled around head coach Ossie Solem, listening to his postgame speech. The Hawkeyes were now 1-3 on the season, and their schedule didn't get any easier.

Dutch smiled as he thought fondly of his football playing days, first in high school in Dixon, Illinois, then at Eureka College. Why, he wasn't much older than the boys on the field in front of him, but now, with a college degree under his belt, Dutch suddenly felt quite mature.

"Alright, Dutch, here's your five dollars," said the station manager. "You did a good job today . . . a real good job considering that was your first official broadcast. You're hired."

Dutch was elated. He had graduated from college the previous June, and this gig of doing play-by-play for WOC Radio of Davenport in late October was his first real job. And he even got paid five whole dollars to do it!

Ronald "Dutch" Reagan was on his way.

Ronald Reagan was born on February 6, 1911, to Nelle and Jack Reagan of Tampico, Illinois. The Reagans moved often when Ronald was young, finally settling in Dixon, Illinois, when he was nine.

Jack worked as a shoe salesman and Nelle was a part-time preacher for the Disciples of Christ Church. The young Reagan grew up memorizing Bible passages and going on house calls and jail visits with his mother. He would also help his mother with her sermons and performed in morality plays she wrote. In high school, Reagan became a lifeguard and, in addition to playing football, performed in most of the school's dramatic offerings.

Reagan attended college at Eureka College in Eureka, Illinois, where he majored in economics. He was elected student body president and played football all four years, lettering in the sport. On the weekends, he would return to Dixon to teach Sunday School.

When Reagan graduated in June 1932, he knew deep down that he wanted to go to Hollywood to be an actor. However, he didn't feel that a career that frivolous was a good idea to pursue when the country was in the middle of the Great Depression. Instead, Reagan decided to break into radio.

Radio was still fairly new in 1932, and having a radio at home was a trend that was picking up steam across the country, even though stations were limited to the bigger cities. Reagan traveled to Chicago right after graduation and applied at every station he could find. They all turned him down, but one station manager recommended that Reagan get some experience in "the sticks," meaning in smaller cities in Illinois or Iowa.

Reagan took the advice to heart and headed to Davenport, Iowa. Reagan had heard of WOC Radio; it had started in 1922 as the first station west of the Mississippi River. Owned by B. J. Palmer of Davenport's Palmer School of Chiropractic, WOC broadcasted weather reports, farm information, stock prices, and collegiate sports.

Reagan approached WOC with the intent of taking any job just to get his foot in the door. When asked if he knew anything about football, he told tales of his glory days on the fields in Dixon and at Eureka College. When asked if he knew anything about broadcasting a football game, Reagan thought back to his days in the fraternity house at Eureka where he did mock play-by-play calls and interviews with his frat brothers using a broomstick for a microphone. Considering that as enough experience, he said yes. The Iowa-Minnesota game was his audition.

After the 1932 football season was over, Reagan was let go, even though the station had been impressed with his delivery. They just did not have an opening for him. A few months later, however, in the spring of 1933, a full-time announcer position at WOC opened up and Reagan was on board.

In the summer of 1933, just as Reagan was getting the hang of playing records and reading commercials at WOC in Davenport, he was moved to the Des Moines station WHO, also owned by the Palmer Company. WHO had a new fifty-thousand-watt clear channel, making it a major NBC station. Reagan was hired as WHO's sports announcer.

Reagan spent the next four years in Des Moines and became a familiar voice on the radio. He specialized in doing play-by-play for Chicago Cubs baseball games but, unlike most other sports reporters, Reagan never actually went to a Cubs game. Instead, he would sit in the WHO booth in Des Moines across from a telegraph operator. Another telegraph operator would be at the Cubs game in Chicago or wherever they were playing. After each pitch, details about the pitch would be transmitted via telegraph from the stadium to the radio station. The message would be quickly typed up and slipped to Reagan in the booth. Reagan would run a continuous play-by-play based on the telegraphs he was reading and nothing more.

Calling radio the "theater of the mind," Reagan would paint a picture for his listening audience, describing the way the afternoon sunlight fell across Wrigley Field even as he was sitting in a windowless room in Des Moines over three hundred miles away. He would give backstory about each of the players to fill time when the telegraph was slow in coming, and once even made up an entire sequence of pitches when the telegraph line went dead. Reagan called 140 baseball games during the 1934 season.

In 1935, Reagan convinced WHO to send him to spring training with the Chicago Cubs as a way to get more of that backstory. At that time, the Cubs did their spring training on Catalina Island, just off the southwest coast of Los Angeles, California. In 1937, on the annual spring training trip, Reagan spontaneously made an appointment with a Hollywood casting agent. Even though he was enjoying his job as a sports announcer, Reagan still had the desire to be an actor.

The appointment went well, and the agent ordered a screen test for Reagan. Although they liked what they saw, they couldn't commit to offering him any acting roles. The agent asked Reagan to stick around Hollywood, but spring training was wrapping up and Reagan went back to Iowa in time for the Cubs' April 20 game against the Pittsburgh Pirates.

Two days after he returned to WHO in Des Moines, Reagan received a telegram from Hollywood. Warner Brothers Studio wanted to sign him to a movie contract and would pay him $200 a week.

Reagan said goodbye to radio broadcasting and goodbye to Des Moines and headed west. Dropping the nickname "Dutch," he became known only as Ronald Reagan. His first movie was titled *Love Is on the Air*. Reagan played a radio announcer.

During his first year and a half with Warner Brothers, Reagan made thirteen movies. While none were box-office smash hits, most of them did fairly well. During World War II, Reagan made more than four hundred training films for the US Army.

Even as his movie career continued into the 1950s and 1960s, Reagan began dabbling in politics. In 1947, he was elected as president of the Screen Actors Guild, a labor union that represents film and television performers. He also began a habit of campaigning for Democratic candidates seeking office.

In 1962, Reagan changed his party affiliation to Republican and began to consider running for office himself. After his last movie was made in 1964, Reagan took the plunge and announced he was going to run for governor of California in the 1966 election. He won easily and served two terms.

Reagan unsuccessfully ran for president of the United States in 1976, but won by a landslide in 1980. He was reelected in 1984. When he left office in 1988, Reagan had the highest approval rating of any president since Franklin Delano Roosevelt. He died in 2004 at the age of ninety-three.

Ronald Reagan often cited his upbringing and experiences in rural America as the foundation for his life of service. His time on WOC and WHO Radio solidified his status as the country's "Great Communicator," a nickname he was given during his presidential term. Ronald "Dutch" Reagan is remembered today as one of America's favorite presidents.

BONNIE AND CLYDE
AND THE DEXTER POLICE

1933

Just before sunrise on Monday, July 24, 1933, Dallas County's Sheriff Clint Knee spread a map of the area out on the hood of his police car. He gestured for his men to gather around.

"Alright, men," Sheriff Knee began, "we have good reason to believe that Bonnie and Clyde and their gang are holed up here in Dexfield Park."

Knee poked at a spot on the map just south of the South Raccoon River, north of Dexter, Iowa. He then moved his finger to the east a bit.

"I'm going to station a group of you here at the entrance to the park," he said. "I want you to guard the road and bridge and make sure they don't come out that way."

The men, a mix of law enforcement officers and newly deputized citizens, nodded. Knee continued with his plan.

"The rest of us are going to circle around to approach the camp from the west," he said. "That local farmer who found their campsite said they are on high ground here in the south part overlooking the old amusement park."

Knee's posse spent a few minutes asking clarifying questions, and then they got into their vehicles and headed toward Dexfield Park. When they got as close as they dared, they cut their engines and continued the rest of the way on foot. Apprehending America's most notorious criminals was at stake, and everyone knew they would have to take every precaution in approaching the subjects. Bonnie and Clyde were believed to be responsible for over a dozen murders, numerous bank robberies and car thefts, and even two kidnappings. The duo hadn't hesitated to make law enforcement officers their victims either.

Dexfield Park consisted of about twenty acres of wooded hills, much of it dense underbrush. If that farmer hadn't stumbled across the still-smoldering remains of a campsite late Sunday evening, July 23, while out hunting wild blackberries, and noticed the bloody bandages littering the area; and if he hadn't recently heard a radio report saying that the violent fugitives Bonnie Parker and Clyde Barrow were thought to be in the area, there was a good chance the Barrow gang would have gotten away.

As it was, the Barrow gang was just stirring when the authorities were starting to creep closer. Bonnie and Clyde were there, along with William Daniel (W. D.) Jones. The three were making breakfast over the fire. The last two members of the gang were Buck and Blanche Barrow. Buck and Clyde were brothers. and Buck was the reason the gang was hiding out in Dexfield Park.

A few days before, on July 20, 1933, the Barrow gang had been ambushed at their hideout in Platte City, Missouri, more than 200 miles to the south. Law enforcement had been on the trail of the thieving and murdering Barrow gang for more than a year. During the Platte City ambush, Buck had been shot in the head and Blanche had been partially blinded by glass shards. Now Blanche was in terrible pain, and Clyde was worried that his brother was dying.

The gang arrived in Dexfield Park late in the day on July 20 and set about making a camp. Clyde and W. D. went in to Dexter several times over the next few days to get food and medical supplies for Buck. Their getaway car had been shot up in Platte City, and the gang knew they would need a different car when they were ready to leave Dexfield Park.

On Sunday evening, July 23, after three days holed up in Dexfield Park, the gang was considering leaving. Clyde and W. D. got in the bullet-riddled car and drove twenty miles to Perry, Iowa. They spied a 1932 Model A Ford belonging to Perry grocer Ed Stoner and brought it back to Dexfield Park as their second getaway car.

At a signal from Sheriff Knee, the law enforcement posse opened fire on the Barrow gang huddled around the campfire. Grabbing the automatic rifles they had recently stolen from a National Guard armory, the Barrow gang fired back.

In the ensuing gunfight, every one of the Barrow gang except for Blanche was hit. Buck sustained the worst injuries. All five members of the gang took advantage of a lull in the shooting to squeeze into one of the vehicles. The law enforcement posse saw the vehicle attempt to leave the campsite and redoubled their efforts. Clyde, who was driving, took a bullet in the shoulder, causing him to jerk the car awkwardly to the side. The car ran over a tree stump and got stuck. Bonnie, Clyde, and W. D. stumbled out of the stalled car and headed toward the other vehicle. Once they got close to it, they realized the law enforcement posse had destroyed it during the shootout. They would have to flee on foot through the underbrush.

With a quick glance of regret behind them at Blanche and Buck, the three ducked into the trees.

Buck, in the meantime, had toppled out of the car and was lying still on the ground. Blanche was hysterically trying to drag him to cover when the law enforcement posse burst into the campsite. With their guns trained on the couple, the posse radioed for an ambulance.

Some of the posse crashed through the woods trying to follow Bonnie, Clyde, and W. D. In addition to Clyde's shoulder injury, Bonnie had taken buckshot in her midsection and W. D. had been grazed. All three were losing blood.

Crossing the South Raccoon River, the three came upon the Vallie Feller farm. Feller and his family were doing their daily chores and were surprised to see the three bloodied criminals emerge from the cornfield. Pointing his gun at the Fellers, Clyde commandeered their 1929 Plymouth and drove away.

Buck was taken to the King's Daughters Hospital in Perry, where he died of his wounds. Blanche, who was captured back at the campsite when she refused to leave Buck's side, was sent to Jefferson City, Missouri, for trial and sentenced to ten years in prison.

Bonnie, Clyde, and W. D. managed to evade police for the next ten months. W. D. left Bonnie and Clyde and traveled home to Texas. He was eventually arrested and served time for his part in the Barrow gang's crime spree.

As for Bonnie and Clyde, those few days in Iowa in July 1933 were some of the last peaceful days they had. Less than a year later, on May 23, 1934, Bonnie and Clyde were gunned down in Louisiana.

IOWA STATE PATROL

1935

Iowa's Secretary of State Ola Babcock Miller peered over Governor Clyde Herring's shoulder as he picked up his pen. Governor Herring looked the document over one last time and then, with a flourish, signed the bottom. He added the date: May 7, 1935.

"There," Governor Herring said, putting down the pen. "It's official. We have an Iowa State Patrol."

"Excellent," said Babcock Miller. "I will get the word out for applicants right away. I hope to have these fine men patrolling our highways by the end of the summer."

Governor Herring shook his head resignedly. "Ola," he said, "I have no doubt you will accomplish that. You seem to accomplish whatever you set your mind to."

Babcock Miller did not respond as she walked briskly out of Governor Herring's office. She knew that Herring was still a little upset because she had authorized a group of motor vehicle inspectors to start patrolling Iowa's highways last summer without any governmental approval or knowledge. But she also knew the importance of highway safety, and that was all that mattered.

Ola Babcock Miller was known for many things to many different people. She had worked as a teacher and a homemaker. She had entered homemade creations into county fairs. She was an active Democrat and suffragette, speaking out often about the need for social reform. And in 1932 she was elected Iowa's first female secretary of state.

However, Ola Babcock Miller is mostly known as the "Mother of the Iowa State Patrol."

Less than two years into her term as secretary of state, Babcock Miller found herself grieving when she learned of the death of a good friend's son. The young man had died on one of Iowa's unsafe roads in what Babcock Miller thought was a preventable accident.

In the 1930s, most of Iowa's roads were dirt or gravel. More and more cars traveled those roads with very little in the way of traffic safety to protect them. Speed limits were not posted, and although drivers were encouraged to drive at a safe and reasonable speed, that sentiment meant different things to different people. Also, many of the cars at that time were lacking simple safety features such as seat belts, headlights, and, in some cases, brakes.

On August 1, 1934, Babcock Miller took matters into her own hands and selected a group of fifteen motor vehicle inspectors to travel around Iowa and present safety courses to church and civic groups. The main job of the inspectors was to promote highway safety. The group became quite popular and helped with the movement to create an official Iowa State Patrol the next year.

After Governor Herring signed the bill into law, more than three thousand applications poured in. Iowa was still in the grip of the Great Depression, and the idea of a steady job was enticing. Out of those three thousand, one hundred were chosen to train at Camp Dodge near Des Moines early in the summer of 1935.

The training at Camp Dodge was similar to military boot camp and was one of the first police academies in the United States. The men were issued khaki breeches and button-down shirts, knee-high black boots, a black tie, a gun belt, and a cap. For a firearm, the officers were given Colt .38 Specials with a four-inch barrel.

Out of those one hundred trainees, fifty officers were selected to take to the highways for the first time on July 28, 1935. The Iowa State Patrol was also equipped with twenty-seven Ford patrol cars and twelve Indian motorcycles. The officers received $100 a month and had to buy their own ammunition.

Ola Babcock Miller died in 1937 after contracting pneumonia. At her funeral, the Mother of the Iowa State Patrol was honored with fifty-five pallbearers, all uniformed members of the Iowa State Patrol.

NOW PITCHING, BOB FELLER

1936

The pitcher steadied himself on the mound and glanced out of the corner of his eye to first base. The runner on first was crouched low, leaning toward second. The pitcher swung his eyes back to the batter facing him. Bringing his right hand to his glove, he shifted the ball around until he felt the familiar ridge of the seam along his middle finger. He gripped the ball between that middle finger and his thumb and thought about his next move.

The pitcher knew he needed to shift his weight back on his right leg, bring his left knee up and around, and rotate his hips toward the batter as he lunged forward. He also knew that he needed to snap the ball out of his hand at just the right moment to set it spinning for the perfect curveball. But this was his first time on the mound during an actual game, and knowing how to do something and doing it in front of the home crowd were two different things.

It was the spring of 1934. The Van Meter team was hosting Winterset at Oakview Field. The boy on the mound had started the game at shortstop, but midway through this inning, the coach instructed him to take the mound instead. The coach happened to be the boy's father and knew what he was capable of. The boy also knew he was good; he'd been playing baseball for most of his life. In fact, he had spent most of his childhood on this very field, since it was literally in his own backyard.

The pitcher narrowed his eyes at the batter and began his delivery. As the ball flew from his hand, he knew it was going to be a strike. He could feel it. It was, and so were the next two. Bob Feller, age fifteen, had just struck out his first batter.

Bob Feller was born in 1918 and grew up a farm boy in Van Meter, Dallas County, Iowa. His love of baseball started early; at the tender age of eight, Feller taught himself how to throw a curveball. His parents encouraged him in his pursuit to be a better ballplayer. His dad strung a copper wire from the barn to a tall tree in the yard to get the radio signal from WHO in Des Moines so Feller could listen to Ronald "Dutch" Reagan call the Chicago Cubs.

Feller's dad also transitioned from farming corn, which was fairly time-intensive, to farming wheat, freeing him up to play ball with his son. He leveled a spot of pasture on their farm to create their own ball diamond, which they named Oakview Field. They started hosting games when Feller was thirteen years old; he was on a team with men in their late teens and early twenties. Fans were charged twenty-five cents a game, thirty-five cents if it was a doubleheader. After each game, Feller and his dad had to erect a makeshift fence around the infield to protect it from their livestock.

Oakview Field featured bleachers and concessions at a time when the Feller household a few yards away didn't have electricity or indoor plumbing.

Later in the summer of 1934, Feller started his first game as a pitcher against a team from Waukee. He struck out fifteen batters. The following summer, in 1935, Feller averaged 19.4 strikeouts per game. The bleachers at Oakview Field were filled with Iowans wanting to catch a glimpse of the sixteen-year-old phenom.

As the 1936 season began, the seventeen-year-old Feller, who wasn't even shaving yet, appeared on the radar of Major League Baseball. On July 6, Feller was part of a Cleveland Indians exhibition game against the St. Louis Cardinals. With twelve thousand in attendance, Feller started the fourth inning. He pitched three innings and struck out eight. That was good enough for the Indians, who signed Feller to a contract the next day.

Feller joined the Indians for the rest of the 1936 season and started his first major league game against the St. Louis Browns on August 23. Pitching a full game, Feller finished with fifteen strikeouts and gave up six hits and one run. A month later, Feller struck out seventeen Philadelphia As.

In October 1936 Feller's debut season came to an end, and the pitcher packed his bags and returned to Van Meter. Even though he was a rising star in the baseball world, Bob Feller had to finish high school.

Feller was one of sixteen seniors at Van Meter High School that year. He rode the bus to school with his seven-year-old sister, Marguerite. After school, Feller helped his dad on the farm. In February, Feller left Van Meter again to join the Cleveland Indians at spring training. The Indians hired a tutor for Feller, who helped him with his homework every night in the hotel after games.

Feller was able to return home to Van Meter for graduation, but soon hit the road again with the Indians. He made his first All-Star Team in 1938 when he was just nineteen, and pitched a no-hitter to start the season on April 16, 1940. In a baseball era when batting helmets were rarely used, Feller was known for his fast ball; he was called "The Heater from Van Meter," "Bullet Bob," and "Rapid Robert."

On December 7, 1941, Feller, then age twenty-two, was enjoying the off-season when he learned of the Japanese bombing of Pearl Harbor in Hawaii. Two days later, Feller joined the US Navy, becoming the first professional athlete in the United States to enlist. Feller went from earning a six-figure salary as a baseball player to making $80 a month as a chief petty officer aboard the USS *Alabama*.

During the course of World War II, the USS *Alabama* protected supply routes in the North Atlantic and then headed to the South Pacific. Feller was discharged in August 1945 after the Japanese surrender ended World War II. Two days later, he rejoined the Cleveland Indians and played his first baseball game in nearly four years.

Feller continued his baseball career and, in 1948, helped the Cleveland Indians make it to the World Series. Feller pitched games one and five, but did not record a win in either game. The Indians came back in game six to win the series. Feller and Cleveland competed in the World Series again in 1954 after winning 111 regular season games; this time, however, they were swept.

By that time, Feller was reaching the end of his baseball career. He retired after the 1956 season and was inducted into the National Baseball Hall of Fame in Cooperstown, New York, in 1962. Fellers passed away in 2010 at the age of ninety-two.

Feller remains one of the best baseball pitchers to ever play the game, pitching three no-hitters and leading the American League in strikeouts for seven seasons. He often credited his Iowa upbringing with instilling in him fairness, integrity, and the value of hard work.

ATANASOFF COMPUTER

1937

Headlights cut through the cold Iowa night as the car sped down the highway. The driver handled the car competently, navigating the curves and hills of Iowa like a pro.

The driver couldn't say how long he had been at the wheel. He also couldn't say where he was going. He only knew he had a problem to solve, and hours of aimless driving was perhaps the only thing that would loosen up his mind.

The driver was John Vincent Atanasoff. It was the winter of 1937, and Atanasoff was a professor of math and physics at Iowa State College in Ames. The year before, in 1936, Atanasoff had received praise for his invention called a Laplaciometer. Along with Glen Murphy, an atomic physicist, Atanasoff had created the small analog calculator designed to analyze the geometry of surfaces. It was a minor breakthrough in the field of computational mathematics, but Atanasoff wasn't satisfied. He just knew he could create a computing device that was faster, more accurate, and had a larger capacity.

It seemed as though Atanasoff's life had been leading him to this point: driving along a winding Iowa highway in the middle of the night trying to work out a groundbreaking theory.

Atanasoff was born near Hamilton, New York, in 1903. His father, an immigrant from Bulgaria, had a degree in philosophy but worked as an industrial engineer. Atanasoff's mother was a teacher. Both parents strongly encouraged Atanasoff in his educational pursuits.

By the time Atanasoff was nine years old, the family had relocated to Florida. One day, Atanasoff's father came home with a new slide rule. Atanasoff, who had already showed a strong aptitude for mathematics, read the instructions and soon mastered the computing device.

Atanasoff graduated from high school at age fifteen and enrolled at the University of Florida. He studied electrical engineering and graduated with a bachelor's degree in 1925. Even though he received teaching fellowship offers from a variety of schools, including Harvard, Atanasoff chose to continue his career at Iowa State College in Ames.

Once at Iowa State, Atanasoff began work on his master's degree while teaching two undergraduate math classes. By the end of the 1925–26 school year, Atanasoff had earned that master's degree and also gained a wife, Lura. After two more years in Ames, the Atanasoffs moved to Madison, Wisconsin. Atanasoff was planning his doctoral work.

While in Madison, Atanasoff found himself facing serious computing issues while working on his doctoral thesis, "The Dielectric Constant of Helium." Atanasoff was using a Monroe calculator. While it was advanced for its time, Atanasoff wanted something faster and better.

After receiving his PhD in theoretical physics, Atanasoff returned to Iowa State College as a professor of math and physics. He spent hours theorizing about that faster and better computing system. After a particularly frustrating day in the winter of 1937, Atanasoff got in his car and started to drive aimlessly.

Finally, Atanasoff pulled off the highway and into the parking lot of an all-night roadhouse. Pocketing his keys, he stepped into the rundown building and sat at the bar.

"What can I get for you?" asked the bartender.

Atanasoff looked around. He didn't recognize the place. He smiled apologetically at the bartender.

"Sorry," Atanasoff said. "Can you please tell me where I am?"

The bartender laughed. He got all kinds in his roadhouse. "Well," he said, "we're just outside of Rock Island."

Atanasoff looked startled. "Illinois?" The bartender nodded.

Atanasoff had traveled nearly two hundred miles from Ames to Rock Island, Illinois, not even noticing when he crossed the Mississippi River. Shrugging philosophically, he ordered a drink.

As he sipped on his bourbon, Atanasoff felt himself relax. All of a sudden, things became crystal clear. He grabbed a cocktail napkin, fished a pencil out of his pocket, and started scribbling ideas. Words like electricity, binary, regenerative memory, and direct logical action filled the small napkin as Atanasoff's ideas coalesced.

The night in Rock Island, and the long drive there and back, was just what Atanasoff needed. By March 1939, Atanasoff had received a $650 grant from Iowa State College to build a prototype of his computing machine. With the help of graduate student and Iowa native Clifford Berry, the Atanasoff Berry Computer, or ABC, was born.

The prototype was followed by a working model completed in late 1940. The ABC was the first electronic computer and was capable of performing up to thirty simultaneous algebraic equations. At the time the ABC computer was built, mathematicians had only the simplest of calculators to use, with the basic functions of addition, subtraction, multiplication, and division. The ABC computer was a giant step forward in the field of computer science. And, even though it was the size of a large desk, the ABC computer was considered compact for its time. Iowa State College began work on patenting the ABC.

The attack on Pearl Harbor changed everything. Both Atanasoff and Berry left Iowa State for defense-related positions—Atanasoff in Washington, DC, and Berry in California. Atanasoff was named chief of the Acoustics Division at the Naval Ordnance Lab and was soon at work developing computers for the US Navy and becoming involved in the first atomic testing in the Pacific Ocean. The idea of patenting the ABC was soon forgotten.

The war ended in 1945, but neither Atanasoff nor Berry returned to Iowa State College. In the meantime, things were progressing in the computing world. In 1946, the press reported the unveiling of the Electronic Numerical Integrator and Computer (ENIAC). Technology was advancing by leaps and bounds.

Atanasoff continued to work in science, engineering, and research. The ABC at Iowa State had been dismantled and what parts remained were in dusty storage.

In the 1960s, Atanasoff was surprised when he received word that the ENIAC's patent on elements of computer design was being contested. In 1973, after a long court battle, the US District Court in Minneapolis decided that Atanasoff and Berry deserved the credit for inventing the first automatic electronic digital computer.

Atanasoff passed away in 1995 at the age of ninety-one. In his lifetime, he went from mastering a slide rule to creating the basis for modern computers to witnessing the start of a digital world. Iowa State College, now Iowa State University, is proud to have been the home of Atanasoff, Berry, and their creation.

CHRISTMAS AT CAMP ALGONA

1945

Eduard Kaib set the oblong plaster form on his lap and studied it. This was his last piece to carve, and it was, in his mind, the most important one. This was going to be the Christ child.

The plaster was in the vague shape of a child already. The form had been created out of wood and wire, and then covered in a layer of concrete. The concrete, in turn, was covered with plaster. Now Kaib was going to carefully carve the final shape out of the plaster by hand.

Kaib picked up a chisel and, with frequent stops to gauge his progress, began to carve away the excess plaster. The shape that emerged was indeed a baby lying on his back, arms raised toward the heavens.

Near to Kaib in the workshop in Algona, Iowa, were five other men. The six had been asked to create a half-size nativity scene, complete with Jesus, Mary, Joseph, the wise men, and shepherds. They had been working on this project for nearly a year, starting in January 1945. Now, with Christmas just around the corner, the men were pleased with what they had done. Fifty-nine pieces of the crèche were lined up and almost ready for display. All were made of plaster on wood and wire frames. As Kaib was finishing the last piece, the other men were touching up the paint on the others.

Arthur Lobdell stood at the doorway of the workshop and surveyed the scene. He had grown fond of these men and was proud of the work they had done. He cleared his throat and the six men looked up.

"Wonderful job, men," Lobdell said. "This will be just the thing to lift the spirits around here."

The men nodded in agreement. Lobdell walked over to Kaib and held out his hand. Kaib put down the chisel and firmly grasped Lobdell's outstretched hand.

"Merry Christmas," said Lobdell.

"Fröhliche Weihnachten," Kaib responded.

Lobdell turned and left the workshop, stepping out into the cold sunlight of an Iowa winter day. He thought about how different things were this Christmas compared to last year.

One year ago, in early December 1944, World War II still raged on. In Europe, the Allies were on the march through France, and the Germans were gathering for their last major offensive, soon to be known as the Battle of the Bulge. In the Pacific theater, both sides were recovering from the immense Battle of Leyte Gulf in the Philippines, thought to be one of the largest naval battles ever waged.

Now it was December 1945. The war was over, in both Europe and the Pacific. But things were not quite back to normal, as evidenced by the presence of Kaib and his fellow workers on US soil. Kaib and the others were German prisoners of war.

Camp Algona began its service as a German POW camp in 1943. The first prisoners arrived to find a cold, empty shell of a camp and worked hard to make it livable. Within the first year of existence, Camp Algona added a library, theater, and sports facility. POWs organized a camp orchestra and put on concerts and plays not only for their fellow inmates, but also for the American officers who guarded them. The local YMCA provided books, magazines, games, and crafts to the camp.

The POWs also filled the void caused by the absence of Iowa's main workforce. While Iowa soldiers were fighting abroad, the German POWs at Camp Algona worked in local orchards and on farms, in canning factories, and in construction. State officials estimated that POWs completed $3.5 million in work around the state during the war.

Camp Algona soon became a hub for smaller branch camps in Iowa, Minnesota, South Dakota, and North Dakota. In all, more than 378,000 German POWs were housed in the Midwest. In addition to working in factories and fields, the POWs turned to athletics to keep fit, creating their own camp teams for soccer, handball, table tennis, and track. German newspapers were printed at a few of the camps, including Camp Algona, and—although they were lightly censored because of the ongoing war—the papers were filled with critiques on the concerts and plays given by the POWs, reports on sporting matches held in the camps, and cartoons and jokes submitted by readers.

Instead of athletics, Eduard Kaib used his free time to create. Trained as an architect prior to the start of the war, Kaib had been captured and sent to the United States as a POW. In the fall of 1944, he found himself at Camp Algona.

To combat his homesickness that first Christmas, Kaib used the fertile Iowa soil at Camp Algona to mold a miniature nativity scene. He baked the figures in one of the camp's ovens to harden, and then displayed the scene in his barracks. The scene caught the eye of camp commander, Arthur Lobdell, who asked Kaib if he would be willing to create a larger nativity for the entire camp to enjoy.

Kaib rose to the challenge and, using the small stipend he received from working in the area, purchased the necessary materials: wood, wire, concrete, and plaster. Kaib recruited five other POWs to help him, and the six men began work in January 1945. The war in Europe ended with Germany's surrender in May 1945, which was followed by Japan's surrender in the Pacific in August.

The transfer of POWs back to their homeland was slow, so Kaib and his fellow soldiers continued their work on the nativity scene. Joseph and Mary stood by Jesus's straw-filled crib while the wise men approached with gifts. Shepherds were nearby, staring up at an angel singing glad tidings. Sheep, camels, and a donkey completed the scene.

The Camp Algona POWs loved the nativity scene, and so did the American officers and nearby residents. When Kaib was released from Camp Algona and sent back to Germany in 1946, he decided to leave the nativity scene in Algona. His only request was that it be put on free public display every Christmastime.

In the years since the end of World War II, Kaib's nativity scene has become a popular winter destination. Housed in its own building on the Kossuth County Fairgrounds, the scene is under the care of the Men's Club of the Algona First United Methodist Church. It is displayed for the entire month of December each year. There is no fee to view the nativity scene; maintenance of the scene is taken care of by donations.

In 1968, more than twenty years after the end of World War II, Eduard Kaib returned to Iowa. He and his family came as guests of Algona as a thank you for providing the town with the nativity scene. Kaib was not content just to view the scene, however. Ever the artist, Kaib got to work painting a mural of Bethlehem on the back wall of the display. To Eduard Kaib, the universal appreciation of art and the meaning of Christmas far surpassed the impact of war.

THE DAY THE MUSIC DIED

1959

The Winter Dance Party tour was not going well. The Midwest weather in January and February 1959 was especially frigid, and as the musicians made their way by bus from Wisconsin to Minnesota, back to Wisconsin, back to Minnesota, down into Iowa, back up to Minnesota, and back down to Iowa, they were growing tired of the cold weather and drafty bus.

The previous day had been the last straw. One of the drummers had to be hospitalized with frostbitten feet. Buddy Holly didn't want to lose any more of his backup musicians, so he decided he would charter a plane that night. As soon as they were done at the Surf Ballroom in Clear Lake, Iowa, Holly and the rest of his band would hop on a plane at the Mason City Municipal Airport and fly in warmth and style to their next concert destination.

Buddy Holly, famous for his hit "Peggy Sue," had been joined on the Winter Dance Party tour by J. P. "The Big Bopper" Richardson of "Chantilly Lace" fame, and Ritchie Valens, the seventeen-year-old singer of the hits "La Bamba" and "Donna." Holly was the headliner;

he'd been making waves since 1955 when the then nineteen-year-old opened for Elvis Presley. Holly played a mix of country, rhythm and blues, and rockabilly for a very unique sound.

However, he also needed the money that a concert tour would bring him, so he had agreed to do the Winter Dance Party tour, which meant concerts in twenty-four cities over twenty-four days in January and February 1959. Holly asked The Big Bopper and Ritchie Valens to join him.

The concerts themselves had gone well; they were sold out most nights, playing in small clubs and dance halls. But logistically it had been a nightmare. They zigzagged from city to city in an old drafty bus that was prone to breakdowns and had a malfunctioning heater. The musicians were all getting very tired of traveling, and they weren't even halfway through the tour when they played at the Surf Ballroom in Clear Lake on the night of February 2.

Although it was a Monday night, more than eleven hundred youth ages twelve to twenty-one came to the Surf Ballroom, carelessly ignoring the fact that they had school the next day. They paid the $1.25 admission to dance from 8:00 p.m. until midnight.

It was after midnight when Holly and the other musicians gathered backstage at the Surf Ballroom. The crowd had dispersed, and Holly had a private plane reserved at the Mason City Municipal Airport. He planned to take backup musicians Waylon Jennings and Tommy Allsup on the plane with him to Fargo, North Dakota. That was the nearest airport to their next concert stop at Moorhead, Minnesota. The three would arrive in plenty of time before the bus limped into town and would do the laundry for the rest of the performers while they waited.

Waylon Jennings, who would rise to fame in his own right as a country star in later decades, saw that The Big Bopper was still feeling the effects of the flu he had caught on the cold bus. Jennings offered his seat to The Big Bopper, who accepted. Valens challenged Allsup to a coin toss for the last seat and won. The three musicians hopped in the car belonging to the Surf Ballroom manager and sped to the airport.

Meanwhile, Roger Peterson was readying the Beech Bonanza N3794N at the Mason City Municipal Airport. Peterson, who was only twenty-one years old, had been flying for several years and was currently a commercial pilot and flight instructor for the Dwyer Flying Service. Part of Peterson's readying routine was to check with the air traffic communications station in the airport tower for updated weather conditions. Reports indicated that a cold front was on the way, but visibility was still ten miles. Peterson decided to go ahead with the flight. He completed his preflight check as a light snow started falling.

Around 12:40 a.m., Holly, The Big Bopper, and Valens arrived at the airport and boarded the plane. One last check of the weather indicated visibility had dropped to six miles. The wind was picking up and it was below freezing. The Beech Bonanza taxied to the north end of the runway, turned, and idled. At 1:00 a.m., the plane took off toward the south. As it rose into the air, Peterson steered the plane into a gradual 180-degree turn and continued on in a northwesterly direction.

On the ground at the Mason City Municipal Airport, witnesses observed the red taillight of the Beech Bonanza start to slowly descend and disappear. Concerned, the witnesses attempted to reach Peterson via the radio. There was no response.

As soon as it was light enough the next morning, search crews were sent out to look for the plane. One crew hopped in a plane to retrace the route. Just after 9:30 a.m. on February 3, the wreckage of Beech Bonanza N3794N was spotted in a remote cornfield on the Albert Juhl farm, five miles northwest of the airport. All three passengers had been thrown clear of the crash, but none survived. Peterson, the pilot, was still in the cockpit. He also did not survive.

In the months that followed, an aircraft accident report was completed by the Civil Aeronautics Board. The details that emerged from the investigation into the crash indicated that the right wing of the plane had hit the ground at high speed while the plane was in a steep turn. Parts of the wreckage were scattered over 540 feet. The landing gear had not been deployed, and there was no evidence of engine malfunction.

The investigation also turned up two flash weather advisories issued by the US Weather Bureau in Minneapolis that night that were never relayed to the pilot. The first advisory was released at 11:35 p.m. and indicated that a band of snow one hundred miles wide was bearing down on the region. The second advisory, issued at 12:15, before the three musicians had even arrived at the airport, stated that visibility was less than two miles and there was freezing drizzle and fog along with the light snow.

The investigation also turned up the fact that Roger Peterson had failed an instrument flight check eleven months prior to the accident and was certified to fly by visual flight rules only. The accident report concluded that Peterson's unfamiliarity with the plane's specific instruments and the lack of visual landmarks due to poor weather led Peterson to become confused and disoriented. The accident report also called out the air traffic communications station at the Mason City Municipal Airport on their failure to relay the flash weather advisories to Peterson. In the end, pilot error and poor weather were named as the causes of the crash.

The entire nation mourned the loss of Buddy Holly, The Big Bopper, and Ritchie Valens. A stone monument was erected at the site of the crash in the middle of the cornfield and is still visited by hundreds of fans each year.

RAGBRAI

1973

Early in the morning of August 26, 1973, Sioux City residents were intrigued by the sight of a large group of people on bicycles riding through town. Obviously, bike riding itself was not new; kids rode their bikes to school, and families often took evening rides together. These cyclists, however, rode with a purpose.

Some Sioux City residents knew what was happening. Those residents were faithful readers of the *Des Moines Register*. They had been reading the columns of Donald Kaul and John Karras and knew the two writers had challenged each other to a bike ride across the state of Iowa. The plan was simple: The two men, assisted by their friend Don Benson, would take a week to bike across Iowa, from Sioux City to Davenport. They would each submit daily columns about the ride, what they saw, and the Iowa folks they encountered along the way.

Des Moines Register readers were encouraged to follow their progress in the paper. Kaul and Karras published their route and said they would welcome Iowans to ride along with them. On the morning of

August 26, they were surprised when three hundred bikers showed up to join them.

Kaul, Karras, Benson, and the crowd of bikers set out from Sioux City that muggy morning and turned their bikes east. Karras had prepped for the ride by securing a map with daily car traffic counts on all the roads. He had selected roads with fewer than fifteen hundred vehicles per day. Working in an east-by-southeast manner, they made their way approximately four hundred miles across Iowa to Davenport. A trip that would take just under six hours by car took six days by bike.

Of the 300 riders who joined Kaul, Karras, and Benson, only 114 finished with them. Kaul and Karras finished the week tired, sore, exhilarated, and a little glad it was all over. Imagine their surprise when the letters started pouring into the newspaper office with requests to do the bike ride again the following year!

The *Des Moines Register* knew a good promotional event when they saw one and decided to create RAGBRAI: The *Register*'s **A**nnual **G**reat **B**icycle **R**ide **A**cross **I**owa. Since that first ride in 1973, RAGBRAI has continued every year and is now the oldest, longest, and largest bike touring event in the world.

The event has grown from approximately three hundred cyclists that first year to ten thousand today. A lottery system selects eighty-five hundred weeklong participants from all over the world; fifteen hundred more are chosen as day-trippers who complete only certain sections of the trail. While the layout of the ride changes every year, it always runs from a Saturday to a Saturday and goes across the state from west to east. Participants dip their back tire in the Missouri River on the western edge of Iowa at the beginning of the event and finish by dipping their front tire in the Mississippi on the eastern border eight days and an average of 468 miles later.

In the more than forty years since the first RAGBRAI, the event has passed through every one of Iowa's ninety-nine counties and 80 percent of its incorporated towns. Communities at regular intervals along the way are selected as overnight spots and encouraged to get in the spirit of the race by organizing dinners, entertainment, and especially showers for the ten thousand cyclists. Tents are pitched in parks, fields, and even front lawns.

RAGBRAI has faced challenges over the years, mostly in the form of unpredictable weather. Heat, rain, and headwinds take their toll on the participants, and there have been accidents and even deaths. However, plenty of positives have come out of RAGBRAI, including the story of Clarence Pickard. Pickard was eighty-three years old in 1973 when he decided to buy a used women's Schwinn Varsity and join the bike ride. Besides his age, Pickard also had to overcome the fact that he hadn't ridden a bike since the early 1900s, didn't know how to work the gears, and wore a layer of long underwear under his pants and long-sleeved shirt—not the most comfortable attire for cycling in midwestern heat and humidity. Pickard was one of the 114 riders who finished the route that first year. Another positive event happened in 1987 when two hundred riders hopped off their bikes and searched a Worth County cornfield for a lost eighteen-month-old. (They found her.) In 1997, the ever-changing route finally wound through Lucas County in the south-central part of the state. Lucas County was the last of Iowa's ninety-nine counties to be included in RAGBRAI.

Kaul, Karras, and Benson were fixtures of the event for many years after the inaugural RAGBRAI in 1973. One by one, they let others take the lead. Kaul stopped riding after 1982. Benson retired in 1991. Karras's last ride was 2002. The *Des Moines Register* continues to sponsor the event, which has become an Iowa institution.

A REAL LIVE DANISH WINDMILL
ON THE IOWA PRAIRIE

1976

Wednesday, February 4, 1976, marked the dawn of a new era for the small town of Elk Horn, Iowa. For months, the residents of Elk Horn, mostly of Danish descent, had planned, budgeted, and dreamed of this day, and now the time had finally come.

Elk Horn's newest attraction, a real live sixty-foot-tall Danish windmill fresh from the home country, had arrived.

The only problem was that the windmill was in pieces. Hundreds of pieces. It actually looked more like a pile of rotting wood sitting on the back of two large semitrucks than a piece of Danish history.

Some town folk shook their heads and wondered what they had gotten themselves into. Others were so excited about what they saw in their minds that they weren't concerned with what they saw in front of them. Still others, those not of Danish descent, couldn't understand what all the fuss was about.

Elk Horn, Iowa, had been home to Danish immigrants since settlement began in the 1860s. Christian Jensen came to the area in 1868 with his family, a horse, and a mule. Impressed with the rich, fertile soil, Jensen encouraged his family and friends back in Denmark to make Elk Horn their new home. Many did, and the ratio of Danish settlers to non-Danish settlers tipped heavily in favor of the Danes.

By the mid-1870s, Elk Horn boasted a Danish folk school and a Danish Lutheran Church. In January 1910, Elk Horn was officially incorporated.

In Denmark, iconic wooden windmills have long dotted the pastoral landscape. Mills used the natural power of the wind to grind grain into flour and corn into meal. The Danish people relied upon the mills to make their daily bread. Millers had to be skilled at reading wind direction and speed while also being able to maintain the mill in working order.

In 1848, a large wooden smock mill was erected in Norre Snede Parish, Jutland, Denmark. It served the local populace for decades until modern technology rendered the mill obsolete. It served its country again in World War II as a lookout tower and received fire damage. It was repaired but was slowly decaying.

In the spring of 1975, Elk Horn resident Harvey Sornson took a vacation to Denmark. For many in Elk Horn, a trip to the homeland was a pilgrimage to be made at least once. Sornson loved his time there—and especially loved the tall wooden silhouettes of the windmills found throughout the country. The only disappointing part of Sornson's trip was seeing how dilapidated the windmills were becoming. Sornson wished he could take one of those windmills home with him to Elk Horn.

The more he thought about it, the more he liked the idea. Of course, he couldn't really take one with him when he left Denmark, but why couldn't the residents of Elk Horn come together and figure out a way to get one there?

When Sornson got home to Iowa, he presented his idea to anyone who would listen. Having a true Danish windmill in Elk Horn would be a way to honor where the residents came from, he said. It would be a boost to the economy, he said. It would save a Danish landmark from demolition, he said.

Sornson's passion was contagious. The townsfolk of Elk Horn soon rallied behind him, and the donations and pledges started pouring in. In a matter of days, $30,000 was collected for the project. Several Elk Horn residents struck up conversations with distant family members in Denmark and instructed them to search for a windmill.

Within a few months, a plan was in place. Using the $30,000, Elk Horn paid $11,000 for the purchase of the Norre Snede Parish windmill from a Mr. and Mrs. Julius Hansen. Elk Horn paid another $14,000 to a crew of Danish carpenters to dismantle and pack up the windmill. Finally, Elk Horn paid $8,000 to ship the cargo, including the timber, gears, shafts, millstones, scales, and grain carts, from Denmark to Iowa.

There were problems along the way. The $30,000 was gone, yet costs were mounting. Storage charges and customs fees were higher than expected, and issues with transporting the large timbers added to the tally. Elk Horn had to resort to borrowing money to get the windmill to town.

Even once the pieces arrived on that February day, there were more hiccups to overcome. A rough blueprint of how to create the concrete base was included with the windmill pieces, but the measurements had been calculated using the metric system. Also, some of the timbers had been cut to fit on the semitrucks that brought the goods to Iowa, and replacement timbers of the same size had to be secured.

Luckily for the residents of Elk Horn, the Danish carpenters had done what they could to help with the rebuilding. Included in the heap of parts that was the windmill was a six-foot-tall 10:1 replica of the original structure. Each piece on the model was numbered, and each number corresponded with a number attached to one of the actual windmill pieces. All the Elk Horn builders had to do was use the replica as a guide and up the windmill would go.

In all, more than three hundred people volunteered to help rebuild the windmill, including Iowa congressman Tom Harkin. Starting in February 1976, anywhere from six to sixteen people worked on the windmill daily. The construction drew the attention of the surrounding media, and interest was high. Monetary donations to help with the reconstruction started arriving—gifts both large and small. By the time the windmill was officially complete in March 1977, more than $100,000 had been raised. Those donations covered the additional charges, paid off the debt accrued by the city, and even started an endowment. The mill is now operated by the Danish Windmill Company of Elk Horn.

Today, more than sixty thousand people visit the mill annually. It has become a major tourist attraction in the area and even led to the building of the internationally known Museum of Danish America a few miles away.

It is also recognized as the only authentic operating Danish windmill in America, and will most likely retain that title for the foreseeable future. After the Danish government learned about the private dismantling and selling of the Norre Snede Parish windmill to a small town in Iowa, America, they made it illegal to ship windmills out of the country. They wanted to keep these national treasures in their own country.

Of the 650 current residents of Elk Horn, about half can trace their lineage back to Denmark. It remains the largest rural Danish settlement in the United States. Every year, Elk Horn residents come together for a Tivoli Fest to celebrate their heritage under the shadow of the Danish windmill.

BIBLIOGRAPHY

BOOKS

Alex, Lynn M. *Iowa's Archaeological Past*. Iowa City: University of Iowa Press, 2000.

Ambrose, Stephen. *Undaunted Courage*. New York: Touchstone, 1996.

Apps, Jerry. *Ringlingville USA*. Madison, WI: Wisconsin Historical Society Press, 2005.

Beran, Janice. *From Six-On-Six to Full Court Press*. Ames: Iowa State University Press, 1993.

Coffey, Dan, and Eric Jones. *Iowa Curiosities*. Guildford, CT: Globe Pequot Press, 2005.

Feller, Bob. *Now Pitching, Bob Feller*. New York: Sports Publishing, 1990.

Geist, Bill. *Way Off the Road*. New York: Broadway Books, 2007.

Gradwohl, David M., and Nancy M. Osborn. *Exploring Buried Buxton*. Ames: Iowa State University Press, 1984.

Gue, Benjamin F. *History of Iowa from the Earliest Times to the Beginning of the Twentieth Century*. The Century History Company, 1903.

Hastie, Eugene N. *High Points of Iowa History*. Perry, IA, 1966.

Hatton, Thomas J. *Hawkeye Glory*. Fort Dodge, IA: Golden Dragon Press, 2002.

Hersemann, Daryll D. *A Short History of the Lewis & Clark Expedition*. Kearney, NE: Morris Publishing, 2005.

Jacobs, Dennis D. *More or Less Loess*. Lombard, IL: Prairie Fire Publishing, 2007.

Jacobsen, Warren, and Judy Sutcliffe. *Velkommen to the Danish Windmill*. Des Moines: Garner Printing, 1977.

Janik, Erika. *Apple: A Global History*. London: Reaktion Books Ltd., 2011.

Jones, Mary L., and Michael W. Vogt. *Images of America Camp Dodge*. Charleston, SC: Arcadia Publishing, 2009.

Kimball, Donald L. *Heritage & Settlement (History of Iowa Volume 1)*. Fayette, IA: Trends & Events Publishing Group, 1987.

Lehmer, Larry. *The Day the Music Died: The Last Tour of Buddy Holly, The Big Bopper, and Ritchie Valens*. New York: Schirmer Trade Books, 2003.

Ludlow, Daniel. *Encyclopedia of Mormonism*. New York: Macmillan, 1992.

Luick-Thrams, Michael. *Camp Papers*. St. Paul, MN: Traces, 2003.

McElwain, Max. *The Only Dance in Town*. Lincoln: University of Nebraska Press, 2004.

Morgans, James Patrick. *John Todd and the Underground Railroad*. Jefferson, NC: McFarland & Company, Inc., 2006.

Mott, Frank Luther. *Literature of Pioneer Life in Iowa*. Iowa City: State Historical Society of Iowa, 1923.

Palmer, Dr. David D. *Three Generations: A Brief History of Chiropractic*. Davenport, IA: Palmer College of Chiropractic, 1967.

Pellegreno, Ann Holtgren. *Iowa Takes to the Air: 1845–1918*. Aerodrome Press, 1980.

Rasmussen, Chris. *Carnival in the Countryside*. Iowa City: University of Iowa Press, 2015.

Reagan, Ronald. *An American Life*. New York: Threshold Editions, 1990.

Ream, Michael. *Backroads & Byways of Iowa.* Woodstock, VT: The Countryman Press, 2012.

Rosebush, James. *True Reagan.* New York: Center Street, 2016.

Schwieder, Dorothy. *Buxton: A Black Utopia in the Heartland.* Iowa City: University of Iowa Press, 2003.

Southern, Neta Snook. *I Taught Amelia to Fly.* New York: Vantage Press, 1974.

Stock, Janice Beck. *Amazing Iowa.* Nashville: Rutledge Hill Press, 2003.

Zotta, LeAnn. *200 Years and Growing: The Story of Stark Bro's Nurseries & Orchards Co.* Louisiana, MO: Stark Bro's, 2015.

ARTICLES

"Buxton News." *Iowa State Bystander* 12.20 (November 4, 1919): 1, column 3.

"History of Emmet County and Dickinson County, Iowa." Pioneer Publishing Company (1917): 128–29.

Holland, Bernard. "Dvorak's Spirit Returns to the Iowa He Loved." *New York Times* (August 9, 1993).

Langton, Diane. "Time Machine: Old Jumbo." *The Gazette* (February 9, 2015).

Libra, Robert D. "Jumbo: A Runaway Artesian Well." *Iowa Geology 1995* (1995), Vol. 20.

Marshall, Patti. "Neta Snook." *Aviation History 1* (January 2007): 21–22.

Mashek, Robert W. "Dvorak at Spillville." *The Iowan* (October 1958).

Moss, Stephen. "Patriot Frame: the Power of Arthur Mole's Military 'Living Photographs'." *The Guardian* (August 24, 2015).

Nylander, Hazel. "Buxton, Iowa—the Coal Mining Town That Died." *Oskaloosa Herald* (August 3, 1970).

Rasmussen, Chris. "The Man Who Wrecked 146 Locomotives: The Story of 'Head-On Joe' Connolly. *The Annals of Iowa* 70 (2011): 89–90.

Simpson, Pamela H. "Butter Cows and Butter Buildings: A History of an Unconventional Sculptural Medium." *Winterthur Portfolio* 41.1 (Spring 2007): 1–20.

Suddath, Claire. "The Day the Music Died." *Time* (February 3, 2009).

Swartz, David. "Estherville Meteorite on the Auction Block." *Estherville News* (August 15, 2009).

Tegtmeier, Sherry. "The History of the Iowa Girls High School Athletic Union." *IGHSAU* (September 5, 2014).

WEBSITES

www.amhistory.si.edu/archives/d8553.htm. Accessed September 24, 2016.

www.blackpast.org/aah/buxton-iowa-1895-1927. Accessed October 17, 2016.

www.buxtoniowa.com/stories/buxton-wonders-baseball-team/index .html. Accessed October 17, 2016.

www.chamberorganizer.com/esterville/docs/The%20Estherville%20 Meteorite.pdf. Accessed October 9, 2016.

www.chickasawcoia-geniesoc.org/CK_Schools5.htm. Accessed October 30, 2016.

www.co.dallas.ia.us/government/sheriff/history-of-dallas-county/ bonnie-and-clyde. Accessed October 24, 2016.

www.dexteriowa.org. Accessed October 21, 2016.

www.dps.state.ia.us. Accessed September 20, 2016.

www.encyclopediadubuque.org. Accessed October 30, 2016.

www.hooverassociation.org. Accessed October 22, 2016.

www.iagenweb.org/boone/history/kateshelley.htm. Accessed October 23, 2016.

www.iowanationalguard.com/History/History/Pages/Human-Photos .aspx. Accessed October 19, 2016.

www.iowapublicradio.org. Accessed September 20, 2016.

www.iowastatefair.org/about/history-museum. Accessed October 10, 2016.

www.iptv.org/iowapathways/mypath.cfm?ounid=ob_000032. Accessed October 30, 2016.

www.jva.cs.iastate.edu/. Accessed October 21, 2016.

www.littlebrownchurch.org/the-church/history/. Accessed October 21, 2016.

www.muscatinehistory.org. Accessed November 6, 2016.

www.nps.gov/heho/index.htm. Accessed October 21, 2016.

www.powcamp.algona.org/PDFs/Nativity%20Description.pdf. Accessed October 21, 2016.

www.statelibraryofiowa.org. Accessed September 21, 2016.

www.surfballroom.com. Accessed November 5, 2016.

www.wellsenterprisesinc.com. Accessed October 21, 2016.

DOCUMENTARY

Denmark on the Plains. Dir. Anders Birch and Jakob Volver. DR1, 2013.

PAMPHLETS

Brower, Steven R. *Snake Alley.* Greater Burlington Convention & Visitors Bureau.

Estherville Meteorite. Estherville Area Chamber of Commerce.

INDEX

INDEX

ABOUT THE AUTHOR

Tammy Partsch was born and raised in Nebraska. A graduate of Nebraska Wesleyan University in Lincoln, Partsch has worked as a photojournalist, travel agent, bookseller, musician, radio broadcaster, tour guide, and art teacher. In addition to writing, she creates marketing materials for the Nebraska City Tourism & Commerce organization. Partsch coaches the award-winning Academic Decathlon team at Lourdes Central Catholic School and is the piano accompanist for the school's choir and musical. In her spare time, Partsch volunteers on the Friends of Arbor Lodge Foundation and sings in the Belles-A-Peelin' Women's Barbershop Chorus. She enjoys Kansas City Royals baseball, cuddles with her dog, Charlie, and naps. Partsch is happily married to her high school sweetheart, Dave, and is the proud mother of one son, Luke.